CW01629146

" We make no apology for our presence and shouting and fighting to be heard. When you see posts on our social media we make no apologies, we will carry on until we get acknowledged by the people that need to acknowledge us for the changes to take place. "

Sally Nyland

Copyright © 2025 Kathryn Gordon, Guardian of the Book
All rights reserved.

All contributions to this book have been assigned to Kathryn Gordon, Guardian of the Book, with the exception of Kate Rackham's chapter, which remains © the Estate of Kate Rackham and is included here with permission. This arrangement ensures the book can be published, reprinted, adapted into other formats (such as digital, audio, or translation), and negotiated with publishers or partners, while respecting the separate copyright in Kate Rackham's chapter. No part of this publication may be reproduced, stored in a retrieval system, or transmitted in any form or by any means electronic, mechanical, photocopying, recording, or otherwise without prior written permission of the Guardian. The moral rights of the contributors have been asserted. Each woman is credited by name unless she has chosen anonymity.

Proceeds from the sale of this book contribute to:
Sustaining the work of Fighting to be Heard and Funding counselling and emotional support for families facing diagnosis or the loss of a loved one.

First published in 2025 by Kathryn Gordon, Guardian of the Book, in association with Fighting to be Heard (Registered Charity No. SCO52369)

Printed and bound in England
Printed by Custom Print Limited

This book contains personal stories shared with permission. The views, experiences, and opinions expressed are those of the individual contributors and do not necessarily reflect those of the charity, the Guardian, or any associated organisations. The stories are presented as lived experiences and should not be taken as medical or professional advice.

A catalogue record for this book is available from the British Library, National Library of Wales, and National Library of Scotland.

Typesetting and origination by Ava May Tobin
Cover By Ava May Tobin
Original Image by Sane Seven
ISBN 978-1-9192909-0-4

FIGHTING TO BE HEARD

Fighting to be Heard
Twenty women stood together.
A community was formed.
A charity was born.

Hear their cry.
Hear their story.
Hear their fight for change.

CONTENTS

TO DATE

INTRODUCTION

The catalyst was a single photograph. Captured by Sane Seven on 26th September 2021, just after Covid, it told a story without words. Twenty women stood together that day. Within a year, five of them were gone.

That picture changed our lives forever. It was the catalyst for the birth of our charity, a moment when strangers became sisters, and when a shared image became a shared mission.

This book was born from voices that refused to be silenced. Voices of women facing stage 4 breast cancer, of families navigating the unknown, and of a community that came together as strangers and stood together as sisters. Fighting to be Heard is more than a title, it is our truth.

Every story shared in these pages carries courage, grief, love, and resilience. Together, they create a collective legacy of those who fought for change, not only for themselves, but for the people who would come after them.

From the very beginning, we built this movement with no paid staff and few resources, just determination, compassion, and what we sometimes call our widow's mite charity: giving everything we had, with our hearts in the right place. We never waited for "someday" we acted, because we knew what was at stake.

Kate Rackham, one of our co-founders, embodied this spirit to the very end. In her final tweet, she wrote:

"If you're reading this, it means I have died. But do not cry for me. I have lived my life on my own terms, the way I have wanted to."

Those words reached over 1.82 billion people worldwide, a reminder that one voice can spark a global conversation and prove the power of being heard.

Today, around 61,000 patients in the UK are living with secondary breast cancer. They deserve to be heard. Their families deserve to be supported. Their children deserve to have their fears and grief acknowledged.

The sale of this book continues that spirit. Most funds raised will go directly to counselling support for the families of patients especially children and young people. Too often, their voices are overlooked, their fears left unspoken, and their grief unsupported. We know this is a critical service gap. By offering a safe space for them to be heard, we give them the chance to process, to cope, and to carry forward their lives.

This book is for all the ladies we have lost. For everyone who has built and supported our charity. This book is for every woman and man who has been unheard.

CHAPTER 1

THE COMING TOGETHER

September 2021. Just six months post-lockdown, a group of extraordinary women from all corners of the UK converged. Their bond? Each was grappling with the harsh reality of incurable secondary breast cancer. Though strangers at first, they quickly found solace and unyielding strength in each other's company.

The COVID-19 pandemic imposed a brutal reality on cancer patients' fear of travel, compromised immunity due to relentless treatments. Yet, these formidable women were undeterred. They faced the risks head-on, travelling from their homes despite their vulnerabilities, knowing no one, and having never been professionally photographed. Their sheer will to connect, share their stories, and support one another transcended all barriers.

This book chronicles the coming together of twenty remarkable women with incurable secondary breast cancer to create an image that resonated profoundly across the UK. Friendships that grew out of shared struggle, out of loss and laughter, and their individual journeys through the most challenging of times. It also tells of the fastest birth on record of a new charity, launched with a determination and passion that could not be quelled.

Lisa Fleming, founder of Make Seconds Count Charity, reached out and asked if I could turn a National Breast Cancer Awareness Month campaign around in eight weeks. I agreed on the condition that i could carry out the project in my hometown of Liverpool, where I could draft in volunteers, find a location, and tap into my network of creatives. Lisa aimed to create a campaign that would shed light on those living with secondary breast cancer, elevate and spark conversations nationwide, and increase the visibility of the charity. If you know this lady you will agree her tenacity tops mostpeople without an incurable diagnosis, she is a phenomenon.

As I pondered this immense responsibility, I reflected on numerous conversations with secondary breast cancer patients. What struck me most was their aversion to the language often associated with cancer; the terms fighting and battling felt inadequate and misplaced. What they craved most was to be heard, and for so many wrongs to be righted. For people to listen.

The reality was that cancer was always going to win in the end. Their fight wasn't about defeating an adversary; it was about staying alive every day, hoping for another line of treatment to work, giving them precious time. Time to share moments, milestones, and memories with their loved ones.

Thus, the idea for "Fighting to be Heard" was born a name that encapsulated the essence of our mission. It was a call to action to change the dialogue and ensure that every voice was valued.

But reality soon set in, even before we could launch the campaign, some of the remarkable women who should have stood beside the twenty ladies had finished their fight with cancer.

It was a poignant reminder of why our cause was so crucial. We needed to seize every moment and ensure their voices echoed loudly and clearly.

Next came the brainstorming session. How could we visually represent the resilience and spirit of these extraordinary secondary breast cancer patients?

The answer emerged: a gathering in a boxing gym. Not to fight, but to symbolise their unity and strength in the face of adversity. Twenty women from across the UK stood side by side.

The Sane Seven Moment

We needed creative geniuses to bring this vision to life. Enter Sane Seven, a renowned force in campaign photography. Strange as it may sound, the very first time I met Sane, I bought a second-hand coat, one of those slightly quirky ones that you just know has a story. I've loved it ever since, and I always felt oddly lucky whenever I wore it. So, when I picked up the phone and Sane said she and Marius were available and wanted to do the campaign, it was a drop-the-phone, check-the-sky-for-signs kind of moment. It honestly felt like the coat had worked its magic again. Like Lucy stepping through the wardrobe into Narnia, only I wasn't holding a lantern, I was clutching my phone.

We were about to step into something powerful, bold, and a little bit surreal: the world of Sane Seven, where anything feels possible and everything looks iconic.

With Sane and Marius on board, we set off on the adventure that would become Fighting to be Heard, and I had a feeling it was going to be unforgettable.

This wasn't just a campaign; it was a movement a testament to passion, unity, and unwavering determination.

Our mission was clear: to ensure that every voice counted and raise awareness of the little understood incurable form of breast cancer. So, hold on tight. Grab your tissues, a cup of tea, or a glass of fizz, because that's what Sal would tell you to do.

Who's Sal? Well, you're about to love her as much as we did. You're about to embark on an uplifting journey with every lady who has shared their story. You're about to fall in love with them and be inspired, just as I am.

For me, this path wasn't a chosen one; it chose me.

Kathryn

DEFINITELY NOT 2ND BEST
NEVER ACCEPT
MAKE 2NDS COUNT

CHAPTER 2

THE PHOTO SHOOT

There Are Places I Remember

The night before the photo shoot, I was waiting at Lime Street station for Laura Bailey, one of our models, when my phone buzzed. It was a message from her: You won't believe who's on the train, Macca! And then, suddenly, there he was, Liverpool legend Sir Paul McCartney, walking towards me, followed by Laura.

Paul had lost his beloved wife, Linda, in 1998 after her three-year battle with breast cancer. It had spread to her liver, just as it had with our founder, Kate Rackham. Knowing this, I felt compelled to speak to him. It was as though Linda had sent us a sign. Linda, after all, was also a photographer, and I would think she would have been fascinated by Sane Seven's powerful image that would later define our campaign.

I stopped him, despite his entourage trying to usher me away. In the quickest elevator pitch of my life, I told him: We're photographing in Liverpool tomorrow, Paul, twenty women who have incurable breast cancer, just like your lovely Linda. We are fighting to be heard, Paul. We are activists, just like Linda.

I quickly added, here is Laura, one of the ladies with secondaries. She has travelled from London to be part of the shoot. I have never seen Laura in so much shock. He looked me straight in the eye, and in that moment, I felt a connection. Perhaps I caught him off guard, and I only hoped I hadn't upset him. A woman with him stopped to speak with us. At the time, I thought she was his PA, but I later found out she was his daughter, Mary. With warmth and sincerity, she asked where the shoot was taking place and apologised that he couldn't attend due to a prior engagement. She even reached into her purse and offered us some money to help.

I asked her to wait whilst I legged it back to my car for the leaflets. Off I went, darting back up to the vehicles, and handed them straight to Mary. I honestly have no shame. I was polite and not too much of a pest.

As I ran back to the car, Laura filmed the entire encounter yes, we have the evidence. I've often wondered since then if Paul ever heard about our charity. I hope he read the leaflet, if only for a moment.

Linda once said on television: I enjoy life too much to rise above it. I like being on the same level as people; otherwise, you have no fun. I truly believe that if Linda were here today, she would be fighting to be heard alongside us. Perhaps we should send Paul a copy of this book. I think Linda would approve.

And as I think back on that night at Lime Street, I can't help but hear Paul's own words from In My Life about the people and places we carry with us, some gone and some remaining. For us, that will always be the women we fight for, and those we have lost but will never forget.

A Picture Paints a Thousand Words

The air inside the Golden Gloves Gym in Liverpool carried a charge that was impossible to ignore. It wasn't just the hum of lights or the shuffle of cameras being set up it was the weight of anticipation.

One by one, the women arrived. Some came alone, clutching handbags or travel bags, their eyes betraying nerves despite the brave smiles. Others came with family members or friends, who offered quiet reassurances before stepping back to let them face this moment for themselves. Many had never met before. All carried the invisible burden of treatment, pain, and uncertainty. Yet from the moment they stepped through those doors, something began to shift.

Before the cameras clicked, there was the ritual of preparation. Instead of boxing gloves, their hands were wrapped in woven cloth the hidden layers that fighters wear beneath the gloves. Strips of fabric carefully bound around each wrist and palm, holding joints steady, giving strength where there was fragility.

The symbolism was impossible to miss. These weren't just layers of protection; they became a metaphor for the unseen armour each woman carried the resilience built up over years of treatment, the courage to keep stepping forward despite fear. As the fabric crossed over itself, it was as though their stories, too, were weaving together.

What made it even more powerful was the way they helped one another. One woman steadying another's hand, tightening the wrap, smoothing the fabric.

It felt almost ceremonial as if they were preparing not for a fight, but for a shared moment of truth. Strangers just hours before, now binding each other in strength, as sisters do.

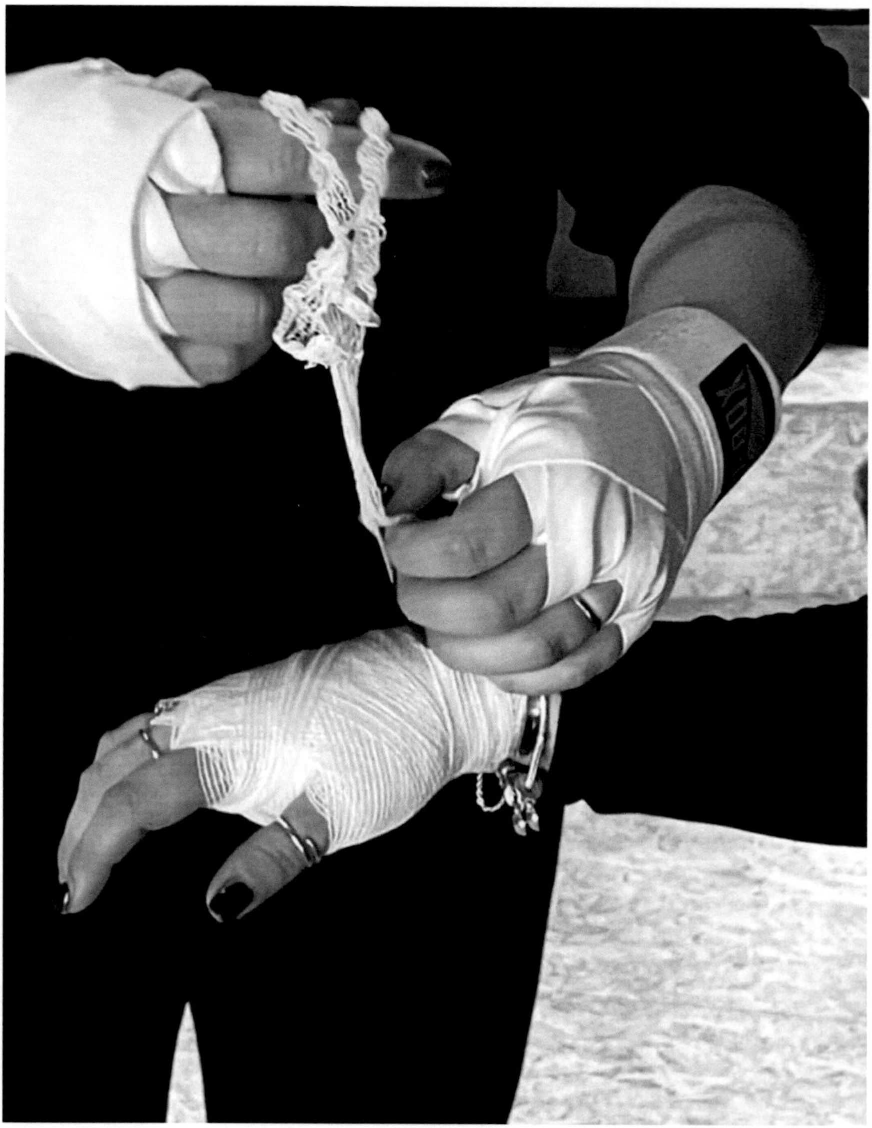

Voices from the Day

"I felt physically sick just before we walked in. I'm a confident person, but the thought of meeting 20 other stage 4 patients, all strangers, was exciting and nerve-racking at the same time. "
Jeannie Ambrose

"I felt immediately comforted and understood." Lisa Jones
"Overwhelmed but proud to have found ladies who understood."
Kimberley Noble

"I was nervous and anxious, by the time I had left, I had a new hope and girls whom I felt I had known for years."
Nikki Williams

Sane - Sane Seven

"As I clicked the shutter on 'Fighting To Be Heard', I couldn't help but feel the weight of what these 20 women represented. Each of them wrapped in the uniform of fighters knuckles ready, but with no gloves to speak of. This wasn't about the glorification of battle; it was about the raw, unfiltered truth of it. A fight where victory isn't in the cards, and yet, here they stand, unwavering.

The image is ambiguous on purpose. Are they gearing up for a fight or have they just finished one? Their expressions are serene, almost hauntingly so. It's this quiet intensity that grips you a stark contrast to the often loud and fierce depictions of 'the cancer fight'. It's in their calm that you hear the loudest call to action. A plea for attention, for research into a type of cancer that's been shoved into the sidelines.

This campaign hit close to home. I've been in the ringside seat to cancer's ruthlessness my husband, my rock, endured the gruelling rounds of chemo for pancreatic cancer. He's one of the lucky ones, standing tall today, but that shadow never quite fades. So, when I was asked to craft this image, it wasn't just a job. It was personal.

But this isn't about my story. It's about these women and the thousands like them. It's for the conversations that need to start and the myths that need to be dismantled.

The photo, if you look at it without context, could be mistaken for a team portrait – a group of athletes, perhaps. That's the double-take moment. It's when realisation dawns, and the true meaning of the image sinks in, that you feel the punch in the gut. This isn't just art; it's a statement, a reality for too many.

In the world of hashtags and fleeting attention, #FightingToBeHe-ard is more than just a campaign. It's a reminder that these women are not just 'surviving' or 'holding on'. They are living, breathing stories of resilience, of moments treasured, and of a fight that demands to be acknowledged not just with words, but with action, with research, with a change. And this is why we need to keep the shutter clicking, keep the stories coming, because as long as they are seen, they are heard. And as long as they are heard, there's always a chance for change."

TYSON
ERGO
ERGO

The gym buzzed with transformation. Makeup brushes danced across faces, lashes were applied with care, hair was styled, and nerves melted into laughter. The space filled with chatter, confessions about treatment, quick jokes, tears that came and went, hugs that needed no explanation.

By the time the women stood under the lights, their hands wrapped, the transformation was complete: no longer strangers, they were sisters in strength, standing shoulder to shoulder in defiance of silence.

Beauty suppliers, who had donated their time and products, added sparkle and glamour to the day. It wasn't vanity, it was visibility. For once, the women weren't being seen as patients, but as powerful, radiant individuals, each deserving of the spotlight.

The cameras snapped, the lights flashed, and something extraordinary unfolded. What began as nerves and uncertainty became courage, and fire in their eyes. Each click of the shutter captured not just images, but evidence of defiance: proof that they were still here, still alive, still worthy of being heard.

This was not just a photo shoot.

It was a declaration.

We are Fighting to be Heard.

GOLDEN GLOVES

Argos
Argos
The
BIG
RED
Event
Big brands, big offer
FIGHTING
PLEASE GIVE GENEROUSLY
THANK YOU!
FIGHTING
TO BE HEARD

CHAPTER 3

THE PATH CHOSE ME

I'm Kathryn, though most know me as Kate, the accidental Chair of Fighting to be Heard, who 100 % never planned for any of this. I was just a decent sales and marketing professional, doing what I knew. But life had other ideas. This path chose me, and once I stepped onto it, there was no turning back.

The chapters that follow are laid out in a timeline of moments that changed everything. Each one brought with it pain, purpose, and unexpected strength.

Years ago, when my daughter experienced a long period of illness, I found myself in a place I never expected, struggling to keep going, emotionally and financially. That experience gave me a lasting understanding of what it means when life knocks the ground from under you.

So, when I later met women living with secondary breast cancer facing not only their diagnosis but real financial hardship, I knew I had to do something. I wanted to be part of a charity that offered more than just words. I wanted to help ease the burden, especially during a cost-of-living crisis that continues to affect so many already fighting so much.

In true Scouse fashion, I stood with the underdog because their fight became mine. You will soon understand why I say underdog, because the wrongs experienced by the ladies in these pages are unforgiveable.

The loss I've witnessed has been devastating. It's taken pieces of my heart I'll never get back. But the friendships I've made with the women I've walked with, laughed with, and cried with have been worth every ounce of that pain.

This is our story. And it begins with a single knowing: that once you hear the truth, you can't unhear it. And you can't walk away from people who have changed your life for the better in every possible way.

THE BEGINNING OF MY KNOWING

My journey into the world of secondary breast cancer began not through personal diagnosis, nor through research or awareness campaigns, but through the life and heartbreaking loss of a friend, client, and young mother, Kate.

I received a call from Kate one I will never forget. Her voice was different, gripped by a fear I could hear and feel. She told me she had been diagnosed with secondary breast cancer.

At that moment, I realised how little I knew. I had never heard of secondary breast cancer before Kate's diagnosis. What followed was a harrowing, heart-wrenching journey, hating every moment of her suffering. She was young, vibrant, and had everything to live for. Yet within just four months, she was gone.

Losing Kate devastated me. My heart remains heavy every time I think of her. She was robbed of her future, her motherhood, her brilliance, her laughter. The world lost a shining light and beauty far too soon. I gained a painful understanding of a disease that, until then was unknown to me.

A LEAP OF FAITH: THE SKY DIVE

For my birthday, my husband surprised me with a skydiving experience. Some people get flowers. I got the chance to jump out of a plane. Now, I'm not what you'd call a natural thrill-seeker. Heights and I don't get on. I couldn't even walk across the bridge at Maghull Station without panicking over the tiny gaps between the steps which gave me a completely irrational (yet very real) fear that I'd fall right through them. So, throwing myself out of a plane at 15,000 feet? That was not my idea of fun. It was my idea of torture.

But I smiled, nodded, and said, "Sure, why not?" because deep down, I knew I could turn this terrifying gesture of love into something meaningful.

Petrified but determined, I took the leap. And as I plummeted through the air, arms flailing, face frozen in panic, I looked nothing like a fearless daredevil. I looked absolutely deranged. When we landed (in one piece, thank God), I didn't walk away beaming with pride. I crawled across the landing field, crying, shaking, I'd wet myself, and felt completely overwhelmed.

Then came the cherry on top. As I tried to pull myself together, an older chap strolled past, laughing his head off, and said to my husband, “She thinks she’s just stormed Normandy!”

The embarrassment should’ve swallowed me whole, but I was so relieved to be back on solid ground, I couldn’t have cared less what anyone thought.

That mad leap wasn’t just about facing a fear. It was a leap of faith in every sense. And it raised awareness and funds for a cause that had become a part of who I am. The money raised went towards launching a T-shirt and hoodie.

Our connection with Seema began during the “Definitely Not 2nd Best – Never Accept” campaign. I had visited New York with her brother on a UK trade mission and she jumped at the chance to support. What began as a gesture of support evolved into an enduring relationship that helped launch Fighting to Be Heard into the national spotlight.

I called on everyone I knew from my days in swimwear, skincare, Mrs Rainbow herself Gaby Roslin who I adore, the gorgeous Lisa Snowdon who I have blessed to know for a number of years thank to a mutual friend, Louisa Bradshaw White a beautiful soul, and Sheena Lynch Seema’s friend who is wonderful soul and supported, more than 100 influencers proudly wore our campaign T-shirts and hoodies to amplify our message.

DEFINITELY NOT 2ND BEST
NEVER ACCEPT
#not2ndbest

DEFINITELY NOT 2ND BEST
NEVER ACCEPT

DEFINITELY NOT 2ND BEST
NEVER

The additional monies raised covered our hotel stay when we gathered for the Manchester Billboard campaign, an unforgettable moment of unity, visibility, and power.

That skydive was chaotic, terrifying, and utterly brilliant. A birthday gift with a parachute and a purpose. And proof that even when you're the kind of person who's scared of crossing a train station bridge, you can still take on something massive and land exactly where you're meant to be.

THE BILLBOARDS: FROM BUS STOP TO NATIONAL SPOTLIGHT

As we tried to gain some outdoor media space for our powerful image, one of our founders, Kimberley Noble, decided to take matters into her own hands. Spotting the advertising company listed on her local bus stop, she picked up the phone and made a call. "If you don't ask, you don't get," never has that phrase rung truer.

On the other end of the line was Glyn Palmer from Bauer Media Kim, with her honest, heartfelt way of speaking, told him about Fighting to Be Heard and the story behind the image. Glyn listened. He didn't just hear it he felt it. Touched by Kim's sincerity and courage, he did something extraordinary.

Bauer Media didn't just offer us a single ad spot; we secured billboards in prime locations across the country. Suddenly, the faces of twenty remarkable women were out on the streets, seen in towns and cities from Manchester to London.

But it didn't stop there.

Thanks to the power of our network and supporters, we also secured free billboard coverage on Europe's largest digital billboard, Manchester Warehouse and several other high-profile sites across the UK. The image was everywhere. The message was impossible to ignore.

We quickly mobilised, encouraging the women to visit their billboards, working with regional newspapers to feature them standing next to their own image in their own communities. The image gained momentum. The conversations were happening. The silence around secondary breast cancer was finally breaking.

Our first major billboard launch took place in Manchester, where I reached out to Lucy Meacock, thanks to Suzy Orr's introduction. Lucy passed the baton to her ITV colleague Tasha Kacheri. Tasha spent over four hours with the women, gently guiding them through interviews and offering emotional support, especially Isla, Emily's daughter, who had just lost her mummy, whose strength was matched by vulnerability. Her ability to create a safe space for truth-telling was a gift to everyone present.

Behind the scenes, Emily Chappell, founder of That Girl Films, filmed for eight powerful hours, documenting raw moments, laughter, tears, and sisterhood. We are now working closely with Emily and her team to turn this into a feature documentary. We just need a sponsor, so if you're reading this and want to help bring our story to the screen, let's talk. If you don't ask...

We were also joined by Seema Malhotra, who showed her ongoing commitment to the campaign with such authenticity and grace. Seema's involvement has helped us reach new audiences and shine a brighter light on the women at the heart of this movement, and we are so excited for her continued support.

That evening, the team gathered at the Brooklyn Hotel in Manchester. Every member of their outstanding staff treated us with care, respect, and kindness, even welcoming us with a fizz reception that made everyone feel special. A heartfelt thank you to Christine Jones for the introduction that brought us to such a perfect setting.

A very special thank-you also goes to the anonymous donor who treated everyone to dinner and drinks that night. Your generosity helped us celebrate the moment with dignity and joy. And to Michael O'Brien, whose Sunborn Hotel voucher helped raise £1,300 toward campaign costs, and the anonymous bidder who matched that energy, thank you.

We had a small gathering in Liverpool, which was mainly for Flossy to enjoy, but unfortunately, she was too poorly and couldn't join us. However, she was delighted that her pretty little face was all over town, and her friends joined us to celebrate on her behalf.

The next celebration was in London, where we gathered at Future Dreams House alongside Glyn from Bauer Media and Sane Seven, the creative team behind the iconic photograph, just as our image appeared in the heart of St Pancras Station. It was surreal. Emotional. And unforgettable.

We were on top of the world, the campaign was building momentum.

And it all began because Kimberley Noble, a brilliant, straight-talking hairdresser with a heart of gold, had the guts to pick up the phone. Her warmth and honesty wrapped Glyn around his finger and opened the door to a national moment of awareness, unity, and power. This is what happens when everyday women dare to ask for more and are heard.

"Kimberly first reached out to us at Bauer Media Outdoor (BMO) in hopes of securing some advertising space at a local bus stop in her hometown. I vividly remember our conversation - she was a courageous woman, balancing the demands of family life and work while facing a terminal illness. She spoke to me about secondary breast cancer and the urgent need to raise awareness through the campaign.

At BMO, we believe we have a role in the communities we serve, being both a platform for brands and a platform for good. It quickly became clear that this campaign deserved a much wider audience. We decided to take it beyond a single local panel and ran it nationally across our digital Out of Home network as part of our pro bono efforts.

The incredible work that this group of women continues to do remains deeply inspiring. It's been a true honour to support their mission and contribute, in a small way, to the powerful legacy they are building."

Glyn, Bauer Media

FIGHTING TO BE HEARD
Make2ndsCount.co.uk
@Make2ndsCount
Clear Channel
FIGHTING TO BE HEARD
Make2ndsCount.co.uk
FIGHTING TO BE HEARD
Make2ndsCount.co.uk
@Make2ndsCount
FIGHTING TO BE HEARD
FIGHTING TO BE HEARD
Make2ndsCount.co.uk
@Make2ndsCount

I WOULD WALK 48 MILES

Tower to Tower – With Blisters, Baileys, and a Cause.

It was after the campaign. After the billboard. After the skydive. That's when The Walk came to life. No big strategy. Just a few friends, a mad idea, and a whole lot of heart.

By then, I'd grown close to many of the women in the campaign. Some of them were really struggling financially. With Christmas looming, I couldn't look away. I'd been there myself: time off work, caring for my daughter and worrying about paying bills.

So, I suggested a walk. Blackpool Tower to Liverpool's Radio City Tower. Through the afternoon. Through the night. Through sheer madness.

We set off: Kate Rackham and her family, along with my amazing friends Rosalie, Ann, Jean, and me. Spirits were high... until we realised, we'd gone eight miles off course. With pit stops fuelled by tea, ibuprofen, Baileys, and my husband's mobile rest and a boot full of moral support, we pressed on.

At 6 am, just when our legs and spirits were flagging, Kate Enell appeared like a vision after a night out, still slightly tipsy but determined, as she felt total FOMO not being there sooner. She walked 16 miles with us while living with secondary breast cancer that had spread to her liver and brain. That kind of strength and Kate's spirit is what our charity is built on.

Sean Snape had joined us at the start, then headed home... or so we thought. After a nap in the car, he reappeared at my mum's house, just in time for egg butties. Perfect timing. From there, we carried on to my dad's pub, where a few Tequila Rose shots gave us the kick we needed to push through the final miles.

The damage tally? Rosalie finished with drop foot. My hips have never been the same. Annie was hallucinating (we still don't know what she saw). And Jean? Jean could've walked another 40 miles without blinking.

As we entered Liverpool, we linked arms and walked the final stretch hand in hand, greeted by friends, family, and a sea of cheers, hugs, and happy tears.

The funds we raised. They helped support the women over Christmas, and there was even enough left to cover the hotel rooms for our official charity launch in Manchester, which at the time we didn't even know was in front of us.

It was never just a walk. It was a statement. A movement.

Rosalie Galvin

Rosalie is not only a dear friend but also one of our most cherished ambassadors. She has been by the community's side from even before the charity was created, and we are so grateful for her love, her energy, and of course her voice of an angel, which has entertained and uplifted our supporters at every event.

In Rosalie's own words:

"My first memory of breast cancer was when I was around ten years of age, when a neighbour and close family friend was diagnosed. I remember her always telling us to look after ourselves, and she would even show us her false breast that she didn't ever wear. Unfortunately, her cancer came back as secondary, and she passed away.

I live in a large community in Liverpool called Kirkby, and I feel that in the last few years breast cancer has become more common in women, particularly young women. I won't go into naming people at this point, but some ladies who I call close friends - and one of my best friends - have been diagnosed with breast cancer. Luckily, the treatments have worked, and we still have these ladies here with us.

I became involved in the breast cancer community through a close friend, Kathryn Orr, who was working alongside a friend on a skincare brand. She went on to become involved with a network of ladies who all have secondary breast cancer. An idea came to highlight secondary breast cancer, as a lot of women and men are fighting to be heard every day, and a charity was set up.

I took part in a walk from Blackpool to Liverpool to raise funds to launch the charity, and I have been proudly involved ever since attending the official launch in Manchester, then on to the first fundraising ball in Chester, and most recently the event at Gaucho Liverpool. I'm extremely lucky to call all involved my friends."

I will never forget one moment from the walk. In the small hours of the morning, when the cold and exhaustion felt overwhelming, something extraordinary happened. From deep inside my bag, a song suddenly began to play on my phone: "I'll Stand by You" by The Pretenders. Rosalie and I stopped and looked at each other in total shock. This was our anthem. In that instant, it felt like we were being sent a message of strength and love to carry us through.

That memory has never left me. It reminds me, always, that even in our darkest hours, we are never truly alone.

CHAPTER 4

THE BIRTH OF OUR CHARITY

THE SPIRIT OF SAL

On the day of Sal's funeral, a vision was imagined that would forever change our lives. Amidst the profound sorrow, a group of us decided to honour Sal's memory by continuing her legacy through the creation of a charity.

The Spirit of Sal what does it mean? Sal was one of the kindest souls on the planet, always making time for everyone, including the children within our group. She had a heart as big as a lioness, filled with boundless love and generosity coupled with immense strength and determination. Sal was not just a founder; she was the mothership, the life of the party with her champagne in hand, our secret fairy godmother, and the foundation upon which our charity was built.

On that solemn day, amidst our tears and reflections, we recognised that Sal's spirit her unyielding kindness, support, and wisdom needed to live on. Sally had given so much to the secondary breast cancer community: love, support, and an immense depth of knowledge. She was an oracle, our confidante, and a friend to our children. She was the wise owl who taught us to 'always leave the light on for our teenage kids.'

Sal's presence was felt by everyone who knew her. We know she is proud of what we've achieved so far and what we will accomplish in the future.

.Our charity's foundation is built on Sal's spirit. Her dedication to serving her community and this earth remains our guiding light. Sal's legacy is one of unwavering love and support, and it is in her memory that we continue to fight for a better future for all affected by secondary breast cancer.

"We make no apology for our presence and shouting and fighting to be heard. When you see posts on our social media, we make no apologies, we will carry on until we get acknowledged by the people that need to acknowledge us for the changes to take place."

CHAPTER 5

THE POWER OF THREE

IT'S OFFICIAL - 2ND MARCH

It started with a call from Seema Malhotra. She told me she could feature a breast cancer charity on The Real Housewives of Cheshire. My first reaction was to ask, "How long have we got until it airs?" When she said, "around eight weeks," I quickly asked if, if we managed to get our charity established in time, she'd let us be on the show because of her connection with the campaign. Without hesitation, she said, "Definitely." I jumped straight on the phone to Gill and Kate, and their answer was just as quick: "Let's do it."

From that moment, everything moved at lightning speed. We received a great deal of help from Euan Fleming, who guided us through the process of establishing the charity; we'll be forever grateful for it. With Kate being a teacher and Gill a magistrate, their experience and professionalism really lent themselves to the formal process of getting everything in place, while I focused on pulling together all the other moving parts. Clarity Creation, who Kate worked for a number of years, kindly gave their time to build our website, and I worked closely with the incredible Seema, Jaya Jackson, and Rae Goddard as part of the planning team for the launch. At the same time, our billboard campaign was being rolled out across the UK, and the momentum was unbelievable. The countdown was on, the energy was electric, and there was no time to second-guess. The three of us were on a mission to make sure secondary breast cancer would be seen and heard on national TV.

We wanted every woman who could be there on the show to have her moment. Together, we encouraged them to be brave, to get up, to walk that catwalk, and to share their voices. Outfits for the catwalk became a priority too. Seema also shared her vision of bringing all the women together for an International Women's Day photoshoot ahead of the TV launch, with the imagery to be used on the night and for the catwalk outfits. Everything was falling into place so beautifully, almost as if someone special was looking down on us.

But by this point, heartbreak had already touched our community. We had lost Emily, Sally, Vicky, Flossy, and Cathy. Their absence was felt deeply, and in many ways, their memory carried us forward. Every decision, every moment we created, was also for them a tribute to their strength, their laughter, and their voices that deserved to be heard.

And so, on 2nd March, Fighting to be Heard was officially born. The charity was founded by Gillian Cory, Kate Rackham, and I, Kate Orr, three friends determined to make a difference. Gill and Kate R, both living with secondaries, carried the powerful insight of what it means to live with the disease. And I, having lost my dear friend and created the original campaign, brought my vision and determination to turn pain into purpose.

We built our charity on three unshakable pillars - the 3Fs:

These aren't just words. They are our promise, our purpose, and the reason we continue to push forward. We built our charity on three unshakable pillars - the 3Fs:

· Fight to Be Heard – we refuse to be silenced. Our voices demand awareness, action, and lasting change.

· Friendship – we are stronger together. A community bound by understanding, support, and the knowledge that no one has to face this alone.

· Financial Support – Cancer is expensive. With so many unable to work, practical help is not a luxury, it's a lifeline.

And between us? Let's just say the 3Fs also had a slightly more... colourful meaning. Not one fit for public record, but one that kept us laughing when life felt anything but funny. I even joked it was better than that famous French Connection advert that got banned. What were they really? Well, that secret's safe with us. But if you're imagining something a little outrageous, whispered over a glass of prosecco, you're probably not far off.

Gill and Kate were made of amazing stuff; no one in their right mind would ever dare cross them! They often told me off for being too soft, and in fact Kate regularly called me her "dickhead." That was our bond, full of honesty, laughter, and love. The three of us became so close, and they made me stronger in every way.

I owe them so much, as do all the patients who have benefited from these two incredible women giving up their precious, limited time for the sake of others.

Can you imagine forfeiting time when you have an incurable diagnosis, just so others could have a better chance? Well, they did. And they will forever be my heroes. And I'll forever be their dickhead.

CHAPTER 6

THE LAUNCH

On 14th March, just 12 days after our charity status was officially passed, we launched at the Menagerie Restaurant & Bar in Manchester, televised for the Real Housewives of Cheshire TV show. To say we were cutting it fine is an understatement. The relief when the paperwork came through was immense everything had been riding on that moment. Without it, none of what followed would have been possible. Seema had invited many celebrities, and I had gathered a crowd of loyal supporters to purchase tickets. The demand was overwhelming we could have sold the night out four times over. The buzz leading up to the event was incredible, and by the time the doors opened, the excitement in the room was electric.

Gill, who I always nicknamed "Joan Collins" because she was the glamour of the group, was absolutely delighted that we were launching on a show she already loved watching. She couldn't wait to meet everyone, and along with the other girls, they were all properly star struck. Kate and I were excited too, but for Gill it was pure joy.

Kate Rackham, in true Kate Rackham style, was the one to kick-start the speeches. With her honesty and strength, she captured exactly what our charity was about and why we were so important to each other. Her words set the tone for the night heartfelt, powerful, and impossible to forget.

Not all twenty of the women from our original campaign were able to walk the catwalk some had sadly died. But those who could, did so with incredible bravery. This was also the stage in our journey where several new ladies joined our charity family. Sukhy travelled all the way from London, even though she was very poorly at the time.

Helena joined us from Cardiff, bringing her warmth and determination. Oge, brought her the biggest smile and energy that could light up the entire room, all the way from London. Then there was the baby of the group, Kate Enell who had been diagnosed De Novo before the original shoot and she had been too overwhelmed to attend, now she was firmly part of our charity and her speech on the night moved the whole room to tears.

The catwalk itself was unforgettable. Gill, struggling with severe neuropathy, was helped to the stage by Kate. Even in pain, she gave her precious time to help start a charity for others. How special. Jackie strutted proudly with her crutches. Roisin brought joy with her rendition of The Boobie Song, and the whole room joined in. Jeannie walked in her frock, but underneath she had slipped on her work boots her trademark spirit shining through. And Sarah, usually so reserved and private, stood bravely on stage and shared her story. Lesley should have been the hired entertainment with her cheeky wit. Lisa and Laura told everyone how fab the shots were! All the ladies had so much fun strutting their stuff especially Nikk who had so been practicing her moves beforehand, the pre nerves were gone and everyone loved being in the spotlight.

Every single woman stood out in her own way, yet together they joined as one in their message: "We are here."
This was the moment. Our charity was real. Our voices would be heard. The women took to the stage, one by one, sharing their truth.

KATE RACKHAM – COFOUNDER, TRUSTEE (SECRETARY)

And in true Kate Rackham style, she was the one to kick-start the night framing exactly what our charity stood for: the 3 F's, Fighting to be Heard, Friendship, and Financial Support.

"I'm 39, and I was first diagnosed with primary breast cancer. Despite surgery, chemo, and radiotherapy, and being told I was all clear, I was diagnosed with secondaries just two years later. I had none of the risk factors associated with breast cancer. I was fit and healthy, the wrong age, I breastfed both my children, and I had no family history. I was told 'it won't be' but it was.

I'm a wife to Mark, a Manchester pub owner, and mum to Ruby, 11, and Nancy, 9. I'm also a full-time teacher. My girls know that I have secondary breast cancer. They know it's incurable, and they know people die from cancer. In my case, my secondary breast cancer followed my primary. Some ladies here tonight were De Novo meaning they were diagnosed straight at stage 4 and thrown into this cancer world.

The symptoms of secondary breast cancer are completely different to primary. My first sign was a pain in my hip, which I thought was a running injury. Turned out, it wasn't.

We want to offer friendship, and a community, to those living with secondaries. Before I met this group of incredible women, I lived in fear and denial. They have normalised my situation with unwavering support and advice. If you are unlucky enough to join our group, you will find love and support like you've never felt before.

Finally, we want to offer financial support to those who can no longer work whether that's paying a bill or making memories on a holiday. It's hard enough worrying about dying without worrying about living as well. Thank you for listening and thank you for joining us in our fight to be heard."

GILL CORY – COFOUNDER, TRUSTEE (TREASURER)

Gill was helped on stage by Kate because her neuropathy was so severe she was struggling to walk and yet, here she was, giving her time to help start a charity for others.

"My name's Gill and I have recently celebrated my 60th birthday. I am married and my lovely daughter is here supporting me, always. I've got a son and a stepdaughter, and I have been blessed with three beautiful grandchildren.

I was diagnosed in 2009 with primary breast cancer. I had a lumpectomy, chemo, and radiotherapy, and after five years of treatment I was discharged and told to go and live my life. They did say it might come back, but at no point did anyone in the medical profession warn me about the symptoms of secondaries or what to look out for. It did come back. It took them eight months to decipher that it had returned in my bones. This was and still is unacceptable. GPs need to be trained to look out for SBC. There needs to be more awareness, and the medical profession needs to be up to speed with it. After all, there are 60,000 of us living with it in the UK.

As you will have noticed, my mobility is really bad at the moment. That is being caused by the side effects of 12 months of IV chemotherapy. It's called peripheral neuropathy I can't feel my hands or my feet. There needs to be more support, more research, and more awareness of these side effects, because people don't understand what chemo can do to your body.

The launch of our new charity today means the world to me and the other ladies. You will never know how grateful we are to have this platform and the media coverage for a disease that is still so largely unknown. The bond and friendship we have formed since 2021 cannot be broken. We will continue to fight to be heard for those we have lost.

I spoke to Seema last year when we were launching the campaign, and she made a promise, and she kept that promise. Thank you, Seema, you truly are unique.

all we

KATIE ENELL – FOUNDER AND TRUSTEE

Our Baby of the Group

Katie was just 30, engaged, and mum to Theo, just seven. We called her our baby of the group, and on this night, she stood bravely before the crowd.

"In July 2021, at 28 years old, with no family history, I didn't know how to check myself or what to check for.

I was diagnosed straight at stage 4. Within two weeks of finding the lump, I was told it had spread to my liver and bones. I went on to have 50 chemo sessions. After a year, I found out it had spread to my brain.

Please don't take anything out of this. Live today, not for the future."

At this stage, Katie broke down on stage, and Seema and Nikki held her either side as she cried but kept going. She even admitted she had rearranged a hospital appointment for a brain scan to be here that night because, as she said, "life is more important. This is more important."

all we
IS

NIKKI WILLIAMS – FOUNDER AND TRUSTEE

Nikki's daughter Charlotte had already sung her heart out to I dreamed a dream, earlier in the night, moving the whole room. Now it was Nikki's turn.

"In 2017 I was diagnosed with primary breast cancer. I was told it was insignificant, had a lumpectomy, radiotherapy, and tamoxifen. I had mammograms after that but no scans, no bloods, no CCTV nothing.

I went back to work as a sister in neonatal nursing. Four years to the day later, the cancer returned and caused spinal cord compression. I had emergency life-saving surgery at Walton Neuro. For two years I had been dismissed when I complained of pain and discomfort.

Five months after diagnosis, I started walking again.

At first, I didn't know anyone else with secondaries. I only had one friend who did. But the day of the campaign shoot, I found my girls. I found a community.

Cancer may have taken away my career, my future, and my health. But it has given me a new lease of life. It has given me a fight and it's Fighting to be Heard. It's given me my purpose.

And I will continue fighting for Emily, Cathy, Sally, Vicky, and Flossy."

LISA JONES – FOUNDER AND TRUSTEE

Lisa shared with honesty and courage, telling the room about her multiple diagnoses.

"I was first diagnosed with cervical cancer, and then a year later, I was diagnosed with triple negative primary breast cancer. After genetic testing, I found out I had the BRCA gene, which made me more likely to have recurring cancers.

A year after that, I was diagnosed with secondaries.
I struggled to get on with my life it was like everything I knew about myself had been taken away. But since meeting the Fighting to be Heard ladies, I feel like I've found my community.

I was told I had 24 months to live, but here I am coming up to three years with no evidence of disease. And I'm looking to get back to work.

Meeting these women has given me a reason to keep fighting, and I'm so grateful."

KIMBERLEY NOBLE – FOUNDER

Kimberley spoke of hope and sadness in equal measure.

"I'm Kimberley, I'm 44 and from Chester. I live with my husband Shaun and our son Charlie, who's 7.

I was diagnosed with triple negative secondaries in 2020. I am currently classed as stable, and my scans for the last three years have shown no evidence of disease.

Meeting the Fighting to be Heard ladies has given me hope as well as sadness."

JEANNIE AMBROSE – FOUNDER

Jeannie stood proud in her frock with her work boots hidden underneath.

"I had breast cancer that spread to my bones, and I was told my average life span would be three to five years. I was diagnosed four years ago.

I have a lovely husband, a son, and a daughter, and I remember wondering how I was going to tell them. But they have got me through this.

Sadly, I've had to leave my job. I had just gained membership as a Chartered Construction Manager, and I was due to graduate this weekend. It is such a bittersweet moment (out came the work boots).

There are very sad and dark times, but Cancer has also given me moments that are beautiful and liberating. Life is now in HD, I see and feel things differently.

I think everyone in this room will have had struggles they've had to deal with. For me, I've learned what I'm made of.

I am proud to be part of the cancer community.
Eighteen months ago, when Sane Seven took the campaign image, we knew it was powerful. And it is for the memory of the girls we've lost, for those who need our support now, and for those still to come."

LESLEY GRAINEY – FOUNDER

Lesley had everyone in stitches and in tears with her honesty.

"I'm married and I shit you not to Mr Rice, Mrs Grainey and Mr Rice!

I was diagnosed in 2018. At the time, my children were 7 and 9, and I was told in hushed terms I wouldn't live more than five years.

I never thought I'd get to 52. But here I am, mind blown.

Now my son is 14 monosyllabic and addicted to his phone and my daughter is 11 and wears mascara to school. I am so grateful to have seen them reach high school.

Being diagnosed with secondaries feels like being pushed off a cliff. All of my hopes and dreams seeing my kids graduate, my career goals were suddenly gone.

To be told it's incurable and life-limiting when you have a 7 and 9-year-old... it feels like someone's pushed you off the edge.

But this community is like the bungee cord. At the bottom of the cliff, that cord pulls you back up. These girls are my bungee cord.

They pick me up when I'm down. There are too many of us with cancer, too many.

all we hair

OGE ONWUACHU – ADVOCATE

Oge brought laughter with her honesty.

"My name's Oge. I am 56, and I have three beautiful children. I went straight to secondaries it's in my breast and liver. I was diagnosed on the 31st of December 2019.

I still went to the New Year's Eve party after I had been told, no one knew apart from my sister until the 4th of January.

I was introduced to Fighting to be Heard through Black Women Rising. Now you are my sisters, because you just get it!

We did a trial run this morning. My baby is now 23, some of you have young children, and I know you're carrying a lot. For me, I just have to look after myself, I feel for all the mums with young ones having to navigate the demands of a young family along with this diagnosis.

I'm glad I've made friends here for the rest of the time I have left, I don't mean to be miserable. I'm still working full time in fact, I bunked off work to come here. Thank you, Karen,... hahaha, I mean Kathryn! Why do I keep calling Kathryn, Karen?"

The whole room erupted with laughter.

all we
IS

ROISIN PELAN – FOUNDER

Roisin had the whole room smiling from the start. 41, full of life, and the kind of woman who could make you laugh even when she was sharing the hardest truths.

"I was diagnosed while pregnant with my little dream boat, Ivy Brown. A lot of people don't know this, but when you're pregnant, the hormones your body produces can actually encourage cancer to grow. That's why I've been working on a leaflet that's now being shared across the Northwest in hospitals, encouraging women to check for any lumps or changes while pregnant. Three years after my original diagnosis, the bugger came back. My daughter was three, and there was no way on planet earth I was going to be able to leave her she's my little bestie, and she still is.

I had to push for second opinions. They told me to 'aim for three years' and even asked on the day of my diagnosis if I wanted help writing my will. That's how much people with secondaries can feel written off.

They also told us we wouldn't be able to adopt. But yesterday, I got a clear scan and I got my little boy as well. And now we are going to sing the song we do at shower time! Come on all join in."

Roisin's Boobie Song Wave your hands up in the air, Wave them round like you just don't care, Now check for lumps upon your chest, Under your arms and in your neck. Now give yourself a great big smile, Your check's all done for a little while.

SARAH LARNER – FOUNDER

Sarah's voice was calm but carried the full weight of her truth.

"I was 34 when I was diagnosed, four years ago. I was on maternity leave from my job as a Clinical Specialist Physiotherapist. Whilst breastfeeding my six-month-old baby, she suddenly became quite fussy. That's when I found a small lump. I went to my GP, and the surgeon said it was likely nothing to worry about. But then the tests came back and my whole world came crashing down. I was told I had stage 4 incurable breast cancer. That it would shorten my life expectancy.

At a time when I should have been enjoying my little girl, I was being told I might not see her start school, let alone graduate, drive, or start a family of her own.

I'd had a healthy pregnancy, problem free. I even played rugby while pregnant and had recently climbed Kilimanjaro. There were no red flags, no symptoms, just a small lump.Who knows their boobs better than a breastfeeding mum?

But my cancer has not stayed sleeping. I am now on my third line of treatment, and there aren't many left for me to try.

That's why Fighting to be Heard matters so much. We need more treatment options, and we need more time.

I am grateful for your support."

all we have
IS NO

JACKIE – FOUNDER

Jackie, who later strutted the catwalk proudly with her crutches, reminded us all her extraordinary two decades of resilience.

"I am 52, and I have lived with breast cancer for twenty years now. I was initially diagnosed in 2002, when I was just 32, with primary breast cancer. I didn't think I would live to forty, never mind fifty.

Unfortunately, 17 years after my primary diagnosis when I thought cancer was part of my history I was diagnosed with secondary breast cancer.

I needed radical surgery, and it changed my life. I now use either a wheelchair or crutches.

But I am still here, and I am still thriving.

That's thanks to these lovely ladies, and the support of so many people."

all we have
IS NOW

HELENA AWUAKYE – ADVOCATE

Helena's nerves were clear at the start - but her words rang out strong.

"Bear with me because I am really nervous. I'm a proud mum to Josh, who is 22. I was diagnosed in July 2021. Initially I was told it was primary, but after a few scans they suspected it may have travelled to my liver. After my first round of treatment, I was told it was stage 4 and had spread to my liver.

At the start, I was told I'd be having chemo, surgery, and radiotherapy I was in the midst of treatment. But in Wales, if you're stage four, you won't be offered surgery or radiotherapy. That wasn't explained to me at the beginning. It was only when I had my fifth round of chemo, while planning for surgery, that I was told very bluntly: 'Your cancer has spread so you won't be allowed surgery.' That's when I found out that treatment can be a postcode lottery. I think it's so important that we are together, because we get to share and discover the different treatments that are out there. And through discussion, we can fight and say, 'This is available can you offer this to me?'I joined this campaign late. I'm one of the newbies. I was introduced to Fighting to be Heard through Black Women Rising, a charity and support group for Black women diagnosed with cancer. I turned up to the photoshoot and met these amazing women.

We all stand for one thing: to raise awareness, to fight for more options, and to make sure our voices are heard."

all
IS

LISA FRY - ADVOCATE

Lisa worked the floor like a pro,

"I'm 43, a cheeky mum of four boys. Twelve years ago, I was diagnosed with stage 3 breast cancer. I did all the treatment, picked my life back up, became a personal stylist, and even a sergeant in the cadet force.

Against all the odds, I fell pregnant with my miracle baby - the baby I was told I'd never have because chemo had destroyed my eggs.

But towards the end of my pregnancy, I was diagnosed with stage 4 incurable cancer. I had to be induced early, so there I was with a newborn baby and going straight back onto chemo.

I went through aggressive chemo again. But I'm here, I have my life back, and I am living it with everything I've got."

all we

SUKHY KAUR BAHIA – ADVOCATE

"In December 2019, I was diagnosed. I had multiple surgeries, chemo, radiotherapy, and was put on hormone treatment. I was told if I was lucky, we could go for another 10 years and see what happens after that.

I got signed off from oncology in March of last year. Six months later, I was told it had returned this time in my liver and bones.

I am currently off treatment. I'm stuck. The treatment they put me on isn't working. I feel like I'm stuck in a big deep well.

But I am so grateful for the support of these wonderful women to push me, to question things, to ask for the things we need and that we deserve. That is absolutely massive.

Coming from the South Asian community, nobody speaks about breast cancer."

all we
IS

LAURA BAILEY – FOUNDER

"I am Laura, I am 41. In 2017, just after my youngest daughter turned 1, I was diagnosed with stage three inflammatory breast cancer, which is quite a rare, aggressive breast cancer. I went through chemo, radio, and thought I was in the clear. In 2018, I was diagnosed with secondaries. Unfortunately, it had gone to my lower spine, hips every part of my body that is a sore part of a woman, it's there on me.

I was so lonely. Now, I have a massive family and loads of friends. But I was lonely. I didn't realise how lonely I was. See you have done it. Then Lisa Fleming and Kate Orr found me. They took me in and introduced me to this whole community of women that all know exactly what it's like to be told that you can't be told.

All of the feelings of failure. As a mum especially, it is slaughtering to be told you can't be cured. These women, they lift you as women should do for women!

I've just had three shots… It's fine, it's fine. Kate" she looks to Kate Rackham "you little treas. My story mirrors yours, all the markers. I breastfed my kids; I breastfed my little Effy. I had cancer. I didn't know. It's mind-blowing.

It's mind-blowing when you're surrounded by so many people who love you. We are ignored so much in the media, in the press. We are the hopeless cause. We are not marketable. With the big charities we are sidelined harsh but true. Fighting to be Heard is so important!

Have one of the shots, because they are amazing!"

Doll Beauty

FIGHTING TO BE HEARD
X
FOREVER UNIQUE

Doll Beauty

Over 150 high-profile guests filled the venue, including Helen Flanagan, Brooke Vincent, Sally Dynevor, Bhavna Limbachia, and Real Housewives of Cheshire stars Rachel Lugo, Hanna Kinsella, Nicole Sealey, and Lauren Simon. It was a ticketed event, with all donations going directly to the Fighting to be Heard charity.

It wasn't just celebrities who came to show support charities from across the UK attended too, including Leanne Pero from Black Women Rising and Ann Coffey from The Sunshine Group, Aintree University Hospital NHS Foundation Trust. Their presence reminded us we weren't alone in this fight, but part of a wider movement of women and organisations demanding change.

The entertainment that evening was breathtaking. We had performances from Pauline Daniels, Rosalie Galvin, Danielle McDermott, and Natasha Hamilton from Atomic Kitten. There was also a very special performance from Charlotte, the daughter of Nikki one of our founders and trustees. Her courage and voice brought the whole room to tears, a moment that will stay with us forever. Leanne Campbell from Radio City also spoke, paying tribute to her friend Suzanne, one of our ladies featured in the Fighting to be heard campaign and honouring the other incredible women we had lost since the initial campaign began.

The evening itself was hosted by Seema, who, with every ounce of her heart, was behind the cause and the secondary ladies she had already grown so attached to over the two previous events. Her warmth, energy, and commitment carried the evening, and I supported her in making sure every woman had her moment to be heard.

It was an evening that combined glamour and grit, laughter and tears, individuality and unity. Every woman, in her own way, left a mark. And together, they created a moment that will never be forgotten.

The words of our guests captured the spirit of the night:

Bhavna Limbachia said: "I'm honoured to be supporting the Fighting To Be Heard Foundation who amplify the voices of those affected by secondary breast cancer. To all those warriors... I salute you!"

Sally Dynevor said: "I know many women don't feel their voices are being heard. Fighting To Be Heard is providing vital education and support to patients and their families to raise awareness of secondary breast cancer."

Brooke Vincent said: "I feel so honoured to be in a room full of inspirational people and support such an important cause."

Helen Flanagan said: "I admire the advocates of The Fighting To Be Heard charity, it was amazing to meet such strong and inspiring women."

Seema Malhotra said: "I'm honoured to support the Fighting To Be Heard Foundation. I have grown to know each of these women personally and I admire every single one of them and their incredible stories. I am so glad that we are able to use our platform to raise awareness and give these women an even bigger voice."

You've heard how we began, how the charity was born, and how our voices first reached national TV.

What follows are their stories. They contain humour, heartbreak, and truths so powerful they cannot be ignored. Together, they show the reality of living with secondary breast cancer.

Here too, you will hear from the loved ones of those who passed before the commencement of this book tributes to their legacy, their courage, and the impact they left behind. Their voices remain with us, carried in the hearts of those who knew and loved them.

So now, I step aside. These are their voices, their chapters.

This is their fight to be heard.

Angela Preston four-time author and all-round golden lady stepped into our journey with a generosity that words can scarcely capture. She travelled to meet the women in their hometowns and gathered with us at Gill's home, where anticipation and excitement hung in the air. Among us was Laura Shutt, who had first joined our community after the ITV launch. Quietly, gently, and in her own time, she became woven into the fabric of our tribe.

The scene was set with plates of cake, endless cups of tea, and the occasional B&C, Gill's favourite tipple. In that warmth, we leaned into Angela's wisdom. With her encouragement, she assured us that we could indeed do this. Kate Rackham, Katie Enell, Nikki Williams and I sat together, listening, daring to believe we could do this.
I personally felt overwhelmed given the number of moments and events, that had taken us to this place, I began my planning with a timeline to shape the flow and I truly hope it makes sense as you read. I suppose it's too late to worry now.

Angela gave her time so freely, never once asking for anything in return. Her belief in us, her patience, and her gift of guidance became threads stitched into the very heart of this book. For that, we remain forever grateful.

FROZEN IN TIME – 2024

The chapters were written in 2024, when some of our beloved ladies were still with us Kate Rackham, Gill Corry, and Kate Enell. That year was almost too much for us all to process. The heartbreak was overwhelming, and we truly did not know if we could carry on. Personally, I was unsure if I had the strength. The toll on my heart, and the loss felt within our charity family, was immense.

This book was delayed until we found the courage and resilience to focus again. Please bear that in mind as you read the chapters ahead. Some of the ladies have updated their words, while others remain exactly as they were in 2024 frozen in that time, just as we too felt frozen and unable to move forward.

And yet, we did regain our strength. Much of that came from those who believed in our mission, the people who kept fundraising in memory of the women we lost. You may never realise how much you gave us at the very moment we truly wanted to give up. Your support reminded us why we could not stop.

How could we not continue the fight and honour the legacy of our charity family?

On we went, one foot in front of the other.

THEIR VOICES

CHAPTER 7

SALLY NYLAND

Written By Husband Steve

So, our lives changed beyond recognition in June 2019 when Sally went to a hospital appointment regarding what she thought was a 'cyst'. Fast forward three hours later, and we ended up in our local wine bar, in a state of shock. The news that Sally and I had received was incomprehensible. Sally had been diagnosed with triple-negative breast cancer, which is one of the rarest forms of cancer. We drank, spoke and considered how the hell we were going to tell our two teenage boys. This was the most challenging conversation Sally, and I ever had.

Sally started 12 weeks of chemotherapy and a planned single mastectomy. Sally, being Sally, needed to feel some control of this situation and her life; she made a courageous decision to shave all her hair off before it fell out. Sally posted on social media: 'I think I wanted to be in control of something because when you get the diagnosis, you're not in control of anything'.

Sally was renowned for sharing her cancer journey from day one via social media; this helped her to connect with women experiencing similar life events and cancer support groups. It became clear that Sally was developing her own cancer tribe. She posted the good, the bad, the ugly truth and the daily reality of appointments, treatments, emotions and side effects.

Sally was in remission and the doctors felt she was 'stable', but this was short-lived. In 2020, Sally was unwell, and, after further tests, secondary breast cancer was diagnosed. We were told she had an estimated 18 months' life expectancy. It was the most surreal experience, as neither of us could comprehend what was to come. I found myself living one day at a time. Sally created a bucket list, which she named her 'living list'. She was determined to live her life to the fullest; we booked a holiday to St. Ives, which then became our happy place. Sally arranged a day in London with her close friend to go to a live DJ set. Sally always loved a party, music, a drink of fizz, and would often be the last one dancing. We visited two well-known tasting restaurants, and she paired a different wine with each course - how could I refuse?

Sally strongly believed in fighting for treatment for all, and above all, fighting for emotional and financial support for young adults and children whose lives were affected by secondary breast cancer. Sally was often hugely frustrated by the lack of support for partners, immediate children and families. Our lives at home had become a roller-coaster, with Sally sat in the front seat and us behind following her on this horrific journey.

Sally was very vocal in raising the profile of secondary breast cancer through the media. Sally saw on social media the 'Change and Check' campaign; she was the first person to contact them and formed a friendship with Helen Addis MBE ITV Producer (@thetittygritty).

She appeared on the ITV Lorraine show, as she was passionate about raising awareness of breast cancer and ensuring people's voices were heard. She was so strong as a woman, wife, mother and friend; she has passed her strength and values on to us all as a close, loving family.

"Sally was the first person to contact me to say that the Change + Check campaign helped her find her symptoms. She was so committed to sharing the message, even after her secondary diagnosis. Sally was the warmest, most upbeat person who just wanted to help others. Her family were her absolute world but her passion to raise breast awareness was a very close second and I'm positive her work on ITV Lorraine would've helped save many lives. She rocked."

Helen Addis MBE - Head of Features, ITV Lorraine

Sally fought and fought until the last week of her life; she was determined to carry on and ignore the pain. The last two weeks Sally was in hospital, incredibly poorly; the immediate family were by her side. On 21st September 2022, Sally passed away in hospital with me and the boys around her.

Sally's funeral was immense in every sense of the word, such a sad, overwhelming day, but also a celebration of how many people loved and cared for her. 'Her girls,' as Sally described them, were the handful of girls who had been on their cancer journeys together. At the funeral, these girls discussed setting up a charity in Sally's legacy. Fighting to be Heard was formed.

As Sally's husband, I was approached to be a trustee, where I can keep Sally's voice alive. Sally is talked about daily at home, within our close friendships, work friends and Sally's family. Sometimes I feel she is tapping me on the shoulder and pointing me in the right direction.

In Loving Memory

21.09.2022

CHAPTER 8

KATE RACKHAM

My Story

I'm Kate Rackham (46). Wife to husband Mark, a pub owner in our hometown in Urmston, Manchester. Mum to my two girls, Ruby (12) and Nancy (10). And I am a primary school teacher in Stockport.

I was diagnosed with primary breast cancer in December 2016 aged 39. I never expected to hear the words "you have cancer". I had had breast lumps checked out in the past, but every time I was told, "you're the wrong age", "you have no family history", "you are fit and healthy, "you breast fed your children"... "It won't be". And yet there I was with my husband and 3 year old being told I had invasive ductal carcinoma in my right breast.

Treatment for my primary diagnosis was gruelling and made even more difficult with the fact that my girls were only 3 and 4 at that time. But I did what I had to do. Single mastectomy and auxiliary node clearance, chemo and radiotherapy. And that was that. I was cancer free.

"But don't worry, it's not the end of the world." There was the glimmer of hope I needed. Treatment for my primary diagnosis was gruelling, and made even more difficult with the fact that my girls were only 3 and 4 at that time. But I did what I had to do. Single mastectomy and auxiliary node clearance, chemo and radiotherapy. And that was that. I was cancer free.

At that last appointment before being signed off, I remember my husband asking, "What happens if it comes back?" I was angry with him for asking. I had just had the worst year of my life and I was cured, why would he ask that?! The oncologist told us that if it comes back in the breast, I would go through the same process again, surgery, chemo, radio etc. If it came back anywhere else, it would be incurable. I can't remember what the exact statistics were that he told us, but I remember coming away thinking that if I can stay cancer free for 2 years, the chances of it coming back would drop dramatically. I just needed to make that 2 years.

Other than Mark asking during that appointment, we were given no information about secondary breast cancer. About its likely destinations, or about signs or symptoms. We rang the bell and went on our merry way, ready to move on with the rest of our lives.

I never really worried about the cancer returning. Worrying wouldn't have stopped it coming back, and I didn't want to waste my time while I was well. I was far too busy living and making up for the year that I had lost. But that 2 year statistic mark did play on my mind.

It was a couple of weeks short of those 2 years I had been striving for, when I got my secondary diagnosis. I had pain in my hip, which I had put down to a running injury. Luckily, I was on a trial at The Christie, so was being very closely monitored. I mentioned the pain in my hip and they said they would do an MRI scan to be on the safe side. I asked if I needed to be worried about it. They said no, and agreed it probably was just a running injury. They would phone with the results and if it was nothing to worry about they'd tell me over the phone, if it was something else they'd ask me to come in for an appointment.

I was in a staff meeting at school when I got the phone call from a "No Caller ID". I knew it was The Christie. "Hi Kathryn, it's Gill from The Christie. We have your scan results. Can you come in tomorrow?" I knew at that moment that it was back and in my bones, making it incurable.

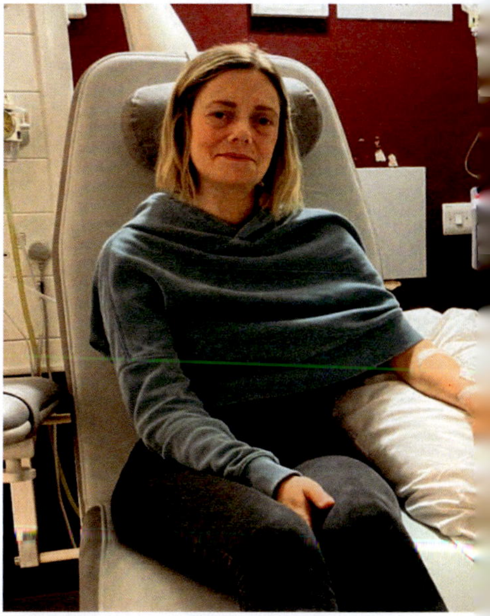

I had never really known what fear felt like until I received my cancer diagnosis. Now The Fear was real and justified. Fear of leaving my family, fear of dying, fear of missing out, fear of being ill, fear of the future. Fear of everything cancer related. This fear lasted a long time. It wasn't always there, but it was never far away, and even the smallest, most innocent thing could trigger it.

I saw an "advert" on the Make 2nds Count Facebook page, asking for secondary breast cancer patients to come together for a photoshoot in Liverpool to help to raise awareness of SBC. Although it was completely out of my comfort zone, I signed up, thinking that it would be unlikely that I would get chosen anyway. But I was, and this was when I met my tribe.

I can't thank Make 2nds Count and Kate Orr enough for bringing me together with these women. I turned up to the photoshoot alone and feeling vulnerable, not knowing what to expect. I had wrongly presumed that I would be one of the youngest women involved, as I hadn't met anyone my own age with this disease. I was surprised to realise that I was actually one of the oldest. I was very much out of my comfort zone. There were some big characters in the room, and I felt quite overwhelmed by the day. I spoke to many of the women, found out their stories - Cancer type, date of diagnosis, age at diagnosis - you know, the usual!

It was very shortly after this photoshoot that we set up a WhatsApp group, and from there our friendships blossomed. We got to know each other well. The group became invaluable. These women were going through the same as me, and they were normalising my situation. Between us all, we were a wealth of knowledge about breast cancer, treatments and side effects. I had well and truly "found my tribe" and genuinely loved these women. The Fear had started to subside.

We met up as a group a few times after that. I loved spending time with these women. They just "got it". We realised that we were special, something truly wonderful had come out of our darkest times. The nature of this disease and our group of women though, meant there was a huge downside. So far we have lost 6 women from our initial photoshoot. Emily, Cathy, Flossy, Vicki, Sally, and most recently Gill. I can't explain how hard this hits and rocks us all. We all know what our inevitable outcome will be, but we focus on living with it, not dying from it.

So when we lose one of our own, the severity and cruelness of this disease is brought into the spotlight. But as tough as it is to lose one of us, we know that we are blessed to have known them and been a part of their life, and that they were one of us. And that makes it all worthwhile.

We had thought about starting our own charity, and talked about it often... "Wouldn't it be great if we could invite more people into our group, so no one has to face this disease alone." We all felt so lucky to have found each other, that we wanted others to be a part of that too.

It was while it was very much in the "talking about it" stage with Kate O, Gill and myself, when Kate O announced that she had spoken to Seema Mulhotra from The RHoC. (We had met her previously at the launch of the F2bH billboard campaign, where she had said she wanted to help us raise awareness of SBC.) Seema had pitched an idea to ITV, who had agreed it and we were going to launch our charity on the show! This meant we had about 7 weeks to go from a group of women talking about creating a charity, to a fully certified charity!

It took a lot of sleepless nights, internet research, calling in favours (thanks Lisa and Euan Fleming!), many, many, many zoom calls, support from our families, but we got there! Fighting to be Heard was born!

We have just celebrated our first birthday! I am so proud of the part I played in setting up the charity, and to be a founder and trustee of Fighting to be Heard. It has taken a lot of hard work to get to where we are, but we have helped over 100 families financially, and have set up a support group. We still have a lot of work to do, and ideas we want to turn into reality, but everything takes time as we are solely run by volunteers, most of whom have secondary breast cancer. But we are making a difference to those diagnosed with Secondary Breast Cancer, and what an amazing legacy to leave behind!

Word of thanks: One of the women who had been integral in bringing us all together is Kate Orr. Not only had she brought us all together, but she became one of us, minus the breast cancer. We are all very well aware that we are a group that you never want to be a part of, but here is Kate O, bringing us together and becoming our advocate. She is an absolute force of nature and I will always be so grateful to her.

Tips:

o Be your own advocate - I can't stress this enough. Educate yourself. Listen to your body. Question medical professionals. Talk to others in a similar situation.

o Know that it always feels better when there is a plan to work towards.

o Set up a blog (I used a secret private FB group) to keep people updated. It can be a full time job replying to well-meaning messages.

o Learn to live in the moment, or at least within scan cycles.

Cancer Type: Er+ and HER2+

My original diagnosis was Er+, with secondaries in my bones (spine and pelvis). Being on Capecitabine for 3 years, I had progression to my liver but my bones remained stable. I had 4 different chemos to treat the liver mets, none of those worked. I was told that treatments were running out, and was referred to the district nurse team and local hospice. I had developed a new lump in my left breast, which was initially dismissed. I had to fight to get it tested (thanks to a school mum friend). It turns out that this was a new HER2+ breast cancer. I am now in the process of undergoing tests to determine the type of breast cancer in my liver. If it matches this new primary, it will open up more treatment options.

Treatments:

- Letrozole, Palbociclib, Zoladex
- Capecitabine
- Paclitaxel
- Nab-Paclitaxel
- Eribulin
- Epirubicin
- Gemcarbo

Kate Rackham

In Loving Memory

12.06.2024

Mark Rackham – Reflection

For the first year of her doing it, I did not understand what Kate was doing on Twitter (as it was called then). Here we were, her close family and friends, seeing her invest so much time into random strangers. We all loved her dearly and wanted her precious time to ourselves, and I have to admit for that first year I resented it. What I came to realise, was that despite our sympathy and loving care, we could not possibly be fully empathetic in the truest sense, of her terminal diagnosis. We did not share that with her, so in that she was alone. Of course she wanted to help others and raise awareness of secondary breast cancer, but a big part of the reason she joined Twitter and started Fighting to be Heard was to reach out to a community that did share that unfortunate and tragic perspective with her, allowing her to be completely authentic and understood.

And wow, look what came of it! In the last few years of her life she achieved so much! We used to joke about tweets "going viral" if they had a few hundred likes, but her final tweet reached 1.8 billion people worldwide through the platform and other media outlets! She would be astonished and delighted! And the media storm and realisation of what she had accomplished by us, her family, really helped in the early days of her passing. We are incredibly proud of her.

I'm delighted to see Fighting to Be Heard continue to go from strength to strength. I know that the values and objectives so close to Kate's heart – around community, compassion, awareness, support and family are still key drivers in all that the charity does.

What a wonderful legacy to Kate and the precious time that she dedicated to the charity when she was alive. And do not underestimate the challenges that come with running a charity where re-occurring grief and loss is part of the deal! The volunteers at Fighting to be Heard are true angels and will forever receive my support. I know with absolute certainty that I helped Kate to be as resilient as she was, and she did the same for me in preparing me for her passing. I can't lie, it has been the hardest thing I have ever experienced, yet it is possible to be grieving and still enjoy life, it is possible to feel deep sadness but still experience joy, it is possible to be a bit broken but still thrive. And for me, our children, and to honour the memory of Kate, I will endeavour to follow her late advice to all that knew her – live a big life, grab it with both hands, run at it!

Poems – Kate & Mark Rackham

My Love By Mark Rackham

Cliched love is a popping stream, a bed of roses,
a galloping heart on a summer's day,
...But my love is different...

My love is loving you as you were then,
as you are now, and every version of you in-between.

My love is time on the wards, panic and fear,
a dark drama that I never chose.

My love is to blame the disease and not the person,
and to remember that it's always worse for you.

My love is to broaden my shoulders, offer strength and
support, as I have no solution.

My love is invaded by an unwelcome trespass,
his grim presence with us on even the happiest of days.

My bittersweet love is noble and true,
it's my absolute privilege to be here for you.

Don’t Be a Dick By Kate and Mark Rackham

Conversations with friends...
A morning at the clinic
With my 3 year old at my side
Whisked off to a side room
These feelings I must hide
Yeah yeah, yeah, it’s fine, fine, fine
But I just want to scream
My daughter eats her chocolate cake
There’s a shadow on the screen You say
“...It’s ok though, breast cancer is the good one to get”
I say “don’t be a dick”

Surgery, chemo, radio
Medical interference
Horrendous fucking side effects
Hoping for some clearance
Just shy of 2 years
When I get THAT phone call
“I’m sorry Kathryn, it’s not what we want
It’s back after all”
You say “...It’s ok though, you might get hit by a bus
tomorrow”
I say “Don’t be a dick”

A career on the floor
And so is all my hair
Can't run or drink alcohol
Favourite foods I cannot bear
No libido and short tempered
Cracked skin and mouth ulcers
Aching hip and lower back
Anxiety compulsions
You say "...It's ok though, you've just got to keep fighting"
I say "Don't be a dick"

And now the end is nearing
The docs have thrown the towel
Liver shot to pieces
Massive, swollen bowel
Yellow skin and eyes
No strength – just fatigue
Saying farewell to my children
Nearly time to leave
You say "...Just stay positive and you'll be fine, new treatments are coming out all the time"
I say...nothing

CHAPTER 9

GILL CORY

After being diagnosed with Secondary Breast Cancer I was thrown into the unknown. I had never heard of it and assumed my primary treatment which included surgery to remove the lump, chemotherapy, radiotherapy and 5 years of hormone tablets had done the job. All I had to do was to have regular mammograms. I was oblivious to what could happen if I ignored the warning signs of Secondary Breast Cancer.

Typically, of me who likes to know the truth and wants to research everything, I did what I had been advised to avoid and that was Google my diagnosis of ER/PR + HER- extensive bone metastases. I joined some support groups on Facebook as I was keen to know how ladies (and men) were coping with their diagnosis and a place I could ask questions. One day I came across an invite by Make 2nds Count to join a group of 20 ladies who would be randomly picked to attend a Photo Shoot in Liverpool to raise awareness of Secondary Breast Cancer. I decided to apply as it was in my area, not far to travel and an opportunity to get my hair and makeup done!

I was very apprehensive when I arrived. The place was a hub of activity, with lots of people crammed into a small changing room. Some ladies seemed to know each other via social media, but I knew no one. What I did notice was that every lady in the room didn't show any signs of Secondary Breast Cancer. They all looked so much younger than me, happy and healthy. You would not know they were all terminally ill. This gave me some reassurance that I was not alone on this journey and had found ladies with the same diagnosis who could become the support that I really needed.

The actual photo shoot was very powerful and very emotional. We had our hands tied, depicting the fact that we had lost our battle, and our gloves were off. Those in the medical profession had failed us, ignored our symptoms, ignored our concerns and in many cases mis diagnosed. Precious times with our families taken away from us. It took very little time to feel at home with other ladies. We each exchanged our diagnosis and how we were coping with it and the effects it had now put on our lives and our families' lives. In some ways I felt guilty as I was a lot older than most of the ladies.

I was very lucky to see my two children Rachel 33 and Jonathan 29 grow up and at the time I had a Grandson Leo 5 a Step Grandson Huxley 3 I now have a Granddaughter Mabel 18 months. I had been married for the second time for 20 years and had lots of happy memories. I thought we had many more to make. Compared to some of the ladies, their children were young. They may never get to see their children go to school, graduate, get married and have grandchildren. These are the things as a parent you really look forward to and dream about, but Secondary Breast Cancer has ripped that away from them, and me.

After the photoshoot, we had a meal arranged at a local Restaurant for those who could make it, to finish off the day. Everyone just gelled. All of us from different backgrounds. Husbands and partners were able to talk openly about their situations. One of the daughters, who was only little thanked us for making her mummy happy for the day. Tragically her mummy Emily Roberts died suddenly not long after the photo shoot from an undiagnosed Brain Tumour. At the end of a long day, I realised I wasn't alone on this journey. I felt privileged to have been a part of this awareness campaign and knew I had found my tribe.

Chapter 2 – Shocking Moments

What I and my family have come to realise is that you must be your own advocate in this Cancer journey. It can be difficult to contact anyone at the Hospital, many times phones are engaged, not picked up or put on hold for long periods of time. This part of the treatment plan can be very stressful for a patient who do not need added stress to their lives. I feel like I'm constantly having to chase for answers and advice. I have listed a few of the shocking moments I have personally experienced during my 5 years being treated for Secondary Breast Cancer.

1. My Initial diagnosis took 9 months to confirm I did have Metastatic Secondary Breast Cancer During this time; I had various blood tests with no conclusion. I was told I could be Vitamin D deficient, maybe it could be fibromyalgia or arthritis. In an effort to reassure me the Breast Surgeon said they were pleased to hear that the pains I was having all over my body indicated it wasn't Secondaries. How wrong they were.

2. Un sympathetic and unqualified Nurses giving extremely upsetting news.

3. I arrived at local hospital to help with extreme nausea. Nowhere to sit other than on the floor and told by a Senior A&E Nurse that Cancer Patients need to sit in an A&E waiting room with everyone else. Cancer patients are very vulnerable and at risk of picking up infections. This didn't seem to be a problem.

4. Given incorrect prognosis when I was admitted to local hospital with numbness on chin. The Gold Standard of Care was ignored. I was told I had a number of lesions on my brain that indicated I had had some TIAs (mini strokes) Asked by a Nurse if I'd been given a prognosis. Next day told by a consultant who didn't specialise in cancer that he had reviewed the scan and there was nothing to worry about and to go home and carry on with my life. He even shook my hand and wished me well!

5. After an operation to place a Port in my chest I was taken to a side ward where I would be observed, given pain relief and information of how to manage it at home while it was healing. I had 1 set of observations done when I should have had three within the hour. I had no pain relief, so took my own paracetamol. I decided to leave as I was clearly forgotten about. I walked out of the ward and no one approached me or called me to see where I was. I contacted PALS who deal with patient complaints. Due to my complaint, I had confirmation the Contract Manager would review the internal transfers and the portering process. Nurses have been spoken to by the Divisional Nurse Director to ensure a better standard of care. No cancer patient should have to deal with this.

7. Being shouted at by a member of the public for parking in a disabled bay. I clearly had a Blue Badge on display. Because some cancer patients don't look disabled, we are often given abuse if we have invisible disabilities.

8. Hospital appointments can over run and often sat waiting for 4 or 5 hours. No facilities to sit somewhere comfortable while waiting.

9. The "Bell" that gets rung after someone has completed their treatment is done within the vicinity of patients receiving both primary and secondary cancer. As I have secondaries, I will never get to ring the bell as my prognosis is terminal. It can be very upsetting to hear the bell and the clapping and cheering. The bell needs to be rung away from those with terminal cancer. It is a reminder of what we face.

Side Effects of Treatment

From the start of my treatment plan I have suffered with fatigue which I have had to manage. If you have never had chemo or radiotherapy you cannot understand what cancer fatigue feels like. It can be debilitating. Your body literally feels like it is deteriorating. At the same time you have to put on a brave face and not show how tired you actually feel. As the treatment progressed and became more intense, I had to face more difficult side effects.

Up to now I have had hair loss, neuropathy in my feet, lower legs and hands. Unable to open bottles or fasten buttons. Neuropathy so bad felt like walking on ice. Unable to walk without holding on to someone. Huge blisters on soles of feet so unable to walk without pain. Breathlessness, losing my balance, feeling very vulnerable and weak. Unable to walk up a flight of stairs without stopping for breath and holding on to something. Weight loss and lack of appetite, loss of taste.

Very often people think the side effects of Chemotherapy is just hair and weight loss, the above is just a taste of what I have dealt with.

Friendship and Support

Some good things have come from having cancer. I wouldn't have met such a fantastic group of ladies from the initial Photoshoot. They are my rock when I am feeling down or anxious. We can talk about everything that we wouldn't necessarily share with close friends and family. I have made friends for life.

I've realised that I need to make the most of any opportunities that come my way. I didn't think that I would become a Founder and Trustee of our new charity Fighting to be Heard Foundation. We are unique to other charities. We want to raise as much money as we can to give direct to Secondary Breast Cancer patients and their families. So far we have helped people with energy bills, weekends away, and money to help with Christmas and Birthdays. It feels good to be able to help those who are struggling. Many patients have had to give up work or reduce their hours to fit around treatments and appointments. Again, this can be so stressful, particularly single parents who have no family support. I have been to some fantastic Fighting to be Heard Charity events supported by local celebrities and businesses. I would never have had an opportunity to meet these people and it highlighted how generous and kind people can be.

When I was diagnosed with my terminal diagnosis nearly 5 years ago I just wanted to know why me? I felt angry towards people who were cancer free. I got fed up of people telling me they hoped I was better soon. Saying the usual " we must catch up soon" and not hearing from them. I find it difficult to look very far in the future. Holidays have been booked and cancelled on numerous occasions due to me being ill or unable to get reasonable quotes for insurance cover. Some quotes are more expensive than the holiday. I feel extremely angry that I am unable to go on holidays now whilst I can and I'm well enough and make those memories I should be able to. It is so unfair.

I look at my Grandchildren and know that I won't see them grow up and I get to see all their milestones in life. Will they remember me as they get older. I'm also aware that I am leaving my children and husband and how they will cope without me. Each Christmas I wonder if it will be my last. Its so unfair. I've had to reduce my working hours from 4 days to 2 days per week. I've had to put on hold my position as a Magistrate, which I love. I feel like everything that I enjoy has been taken from me.

Unfortunately I have to accept my situation. I cannot change it, but while I am here Im embracing each day and trying to think of a positive rather than a negative. I try to surround myself with positive people. I cannot be near negativity, this brings me stress and anxiety. I look back at what we have achieved with the Charity, which will be a legacy for my family when I'm not here, as well as this book. I hope it gives you an insight into what we have to deal with and although I have picked up on what goes wrong,

I also want to say how fantastic the team looking after me are. I am forever grateful that I am being treated so I can be with my loved ones for as long as possible and hope new treatments become available to extend that. Please remember to take each day as a blessing. Tomorrow is not guaranteed.

In Loving Memory

29.04.2024

CHAPTER 10

LAURA SHUTT

"I truly believe everything happens for a reason"

Whilst in the shower on a cold December morning, I noticed a little pea-sized lump which I can only describe the feeling as like a little air bubble. I was already attending an appointment at my GP surgery, so I mentioned it to the doctor. She examined me fully and said she could not feel what I felt, told me to monitor it and come back if anything changed, but reassured me not to be worried.

Fast forward to April and now 10 weeks pregnant I knew the "lump" was growing. I thankfully decided to book another appointment at my GP surgery but asked to see a different doctor. She examined me and said she could feel the lump but it was likely to be pregnancy related although I had explained it had been there since before the pregnancy. She arranged for me to be seen at the local breast screening department within two weeks.

I naively attended the appointment at the clinic alone, reassuring my husband it was just precautionary. I was given an ultrasound, followed by a mammogram and then lastly a biopsy on my breast and armpit. I remember the radiographer asking me what I was going to do with the rest of my day, and I explained I was a teacher and was returning to school to teach the remainder of the lessons. It was at this point I realised the gravity of the situation. The nurses told me to go home, ring my husband and let him know what I had had done and to rest and process the day's events. It was then I began to consider having breast cancer whilst pregnant and started to research previous cases. Two weeks later, and now 14 weeks pregnant I returned to the clinic with my husband and was given the confirmation that it was indeed breast cancer. Stage 2B, grade 3, HER2 Positive, we need to operate, we need to deliver the baby early. All these words, abbreviations and conversations were taking place, but I was in a whirlwind. It was then I experienced what people call an 'out of body experience.' My poor husband Rob was in bits; he literally had the wind taken out of him. We had gone from the happiest moment in our lives finding out we were to become parents for the first time, planning our future, imagining our life as a family of three, to wondering whether I was going to die. Would I meet our baby? Would our baby survive?

6th June 2019 was the day I had surgery. On what was an already stressful day a few events added to that. I met with the anaesthetist and was discussing my medical history before surgery, when I mentioned heartburn during pregnancy. She asked me 'how long ago was that pregnancy?' To my astonishment I replied 'I am pregnant now' she wasn't aware I was pregnant. I then had to go for a scan in the maternity department before they could operate. I was also then told that due to only being 17 weeks pregnant, my pregnancy wouldn't be viable if anything were to happen during the operation and that their main concern was for me and my health. From the moment I found out I was pregnant my motherly instinct kicked in. I wanted to protect my baby; the baby was my priority, not me. I was put to sleep wondering whether I was going to wake up as a soon-to-be mum or whether my baby would not survive the operation.

When I came around in recovery, I arranged for a midwife to attend the ward and she brought a doppler to listen for a heartbeat. I cannot put into words the relief when myself, Rob and my mum and dad heard the baby's heartbeat. Step one complete; I knew I had a little fighter inside of me.

October 15th, 2019, at 7.36am Charlotte Louisa Shutt was born and made mine and Rob's life complete. She was perfect, having undergone a surgery and three months of chemotherapy she entered the world as healthy as any other newborn, albeit a little smaller weighing 4lb 15oz. We started our journey as mummy and daddy and could not be prouder. I was given one week's break from chemotherapy to just be a family and recover from labour.

After six months of chemotherapy, another surgery, 15 rounds of radiotherapy and a year on an immunotherapy drug and a world pandemic within the mix, I finally rang the bell in December 2020 to symbolise the end of treatment and the end of a nightmare. Charlotte had now turned one, had started nursery and I was looking at going back to work as an SEN teacher. I started back at work in March and was loving the normality of everything, the trivial things that we so often take for granted; I had craved routine and was fully embracing it.

15th October 2021 at 5.30pm I got a call to say the cancer was back. Stage 4, incurable, metastatic breast cancer. It was Charlotte's 2nd birthday; we had a house full of family celebrating...

For now, I am doing well. My treatment is working; I received my first ever scan which recorded NEAD last year, which means no evidence of active disease. So, the way I describe it is as if it has gone to sleep, its hibernating. One day it will wake up but for now I need to focus on the positives and hope that the cancer is extremely tired and stays asleep for an exceptionally long time!!!!

I just want to take this opportunity to thank everybody involved in the charity and for the remarkable work we do. The difference it is making to the lives of those benefiting is incredible and so very needed. To my amazing friends thank you, my family I love you. Rob, I could not do it without you, and I know the impact it has on you too, I love you beyond words.

And finally, to Charlotte, thank you for choosing me to be your Mummy, the greatest honour in the world. You have been my reason to fight, to get out of bed and I genuinely believe God sent you to me, to get me through. I will always love you and forever be your bestie my girl.

CHAPTER 11

KATIE ENELL

"Live life for today, as tomorrow isn't promised."

Hello, my name is Katie. I am one of the many Kate's involved in Fighting to be Heard. Whilst I am writing this chapter, I am 32, a mum to Theo, a fiancée to Liam, along with being a granddaughter, daughter, sister, and friend. I feel so privileged that my journey has led me to meeting my tribe of amazing women and becoming a part of this charity. Before my diagnosis, I was a local restaurant manager working for amazing employers who have become family over the last years.

Since my diagnosis, they have supported me in every possible way and given me the option to work in any of the restaurants at any time I feel well. I continued working for most of the first year and a half of my diagnosis, but once the cancer spread to my brain, side effects made it impossible to work. Working for employers like mine has honestly made me realise more businesses should treat their staff like humans and be as supportive as they have been to me – nothing is ever too much trouble. I'd like to give them a special mention in my chapter: So Salsa Crosby, So Salsa Liverpool, Tree House Crosby, Rocksalt Crosby, and Stuffed Crosby. I have worked in all of the restaurants over the years, but when I was diagnosed I was managing the Tree House.

Diagnosis In July 2021, not long after Covid when life was starting to go back to normal, I began to experience severe back and rib pain.

At first, I put it down to lifting heavy tables and chairs when restaurants were still only serving customers outside. But as the pain grew unbearable, I went to the doctors and ended up signed off work for five weeks. During that time, I was bedbound and watching television when Embarrassing Bodies came on. I was about to switch channels when they began showing how to check yourself and what to look out for – early signs of breast cancer. At 28, with no family history, I had never been taught how to check. Not knowing how to check, and never checking, is and always will be my biggest regret in life. Straight away I found a lump in my left breast. Even though my pain was in the opposite side, I believe everything happens for a reason.

Within a day, I had a doctor's appointment. She wasn't overly concerned but thankfully took me seriously and referred me to the breast clinic at Aintree Hospital. I hear lots of horror stories of drs not taking people seriously or big waits, but this was by far my experience at this stage of my journey. Within two weeks I was saw at the breast clinic I had all my tests mammogram and my ultrasound. On the day of my tests, I was waiting in the waiting room between tests and the lady who scanned my with the ultrasound went to the reception desk to ask to book me in for a biopsy the next day and I heard her say something to the receptionist that then said oh my gosh how old is she my heart sank and knew I had cancer from that moment. I was told quite quickly my results from my biopsy that I had cancer and that I would need a CT scan to determine my stage of cancer and if it had spread anywhere else but no one expected it to of spread and thought treatment would be curable and I was told because of my age if I wanted more children I would have to go Liverpool woman's hospital to go through IVF to preserve my fertility it was so hard to make that decision and then go through lots of medication but I was positive I would have a future and I wanted the option.

I was going through IVF and id nearly finished the process when I was very quickly given a date for results Wednesday 30th June at the breast clinic and I was allowed to bring someone with me the minute we got into the room the DR was there along with a breast cancer nurse we suspected we knew I had cancer but in those few moment of sitting down age 28 my life changed within seconds and I was told there would be no point continuing with the IVFD and freezing my eggs as this now was never going to be my future as I was already stage 4 upon diagnosis my cancer had already spread to my lymph nodes, liver and bones at this point making me incurable. My whole life changed all my hopes and dreams of making my family bigger and watching my son Theo who was 6 at the time grow up for two days all I did was cry I could hardly stand and I couldn't imagine a day I could be happy again then on my third day of diagnosis I woke up like someone had switched a light switch and I said to myself I don't know how long I've got left on this planet and I want to make the most of what time I've got left this mindset I've continued to have. Sometimes some days are harder than others, but I find living life this way helps me get through everything.

I then went on to have 50 paclitaxel iv chemotherapy sessions weekly and continued to work and live life with good quality and thankfully my little boy was unaware of anything as he was so young, I wanted to protect him as long as possible. Practically a year later in 2022 I started to get headaches I always found since diagnosis it was hard to know what symptoms were cancer and treatment related but I had heard of many ladies having cancer spread to the brain I pushed for a brain scan for reassurance. I am so glad I trusted my instinct because I had a phone call one Friday at 4pm which would also change my world I was told " Katherine unfortunately your brain scan results are back and I am sorry to tell you that the cancer has also spread to your brain and we have found a tumour in your left frontal lobe". I then had something called SRS brain radiotherapy and thankfully three months later I had a scan and was told the radiotherapy had worked.

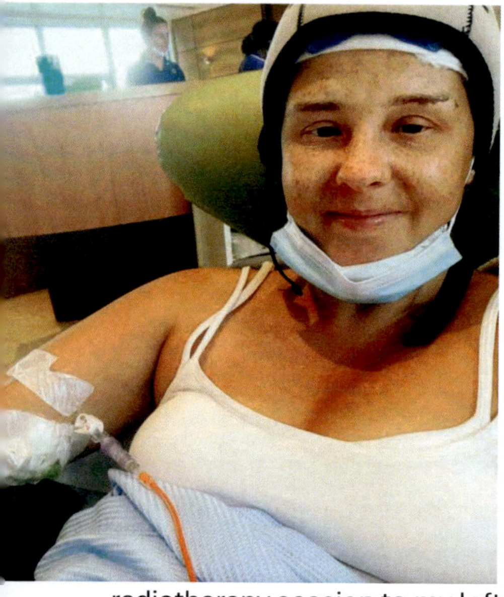

Myself and my team agree that it was best to come of the chemotherapy I was on as it didn't reach the brain and from the neck down my cancer had remained stable for a year it was suggested I stayed on my injection called phesgo and bone injection called detumomab. I had three monthly scans and nearly a year after my first radiotherapy session I was told I now had 4 brain tumours and went onto have another SRS radiotherapy session to my left frontal lobe again were I now had 2 brain tumours and my right cerebellum. Six weeks later I was rescanned to see if the radiotherapy to my brain had worked they decided that the other tumours we thought were new were so small and the brain specialist seemed to think they were there on my original scan but because they were so small they weren't detected and I would stay on my current treatment and be kept a eye on every three months with scans of my brain this gave me reassurance.

I went on to have my 30th birthday and a big black-tie ball to celebrate and I even got engaged and a few weeks later we bought a puppy all three of these things were on my living list and when I was diagnosed were occasions, I didn't think I would see. I should have had scans every three months and life got in the way and by the time I had realised I should if had two scans in the time I was left 9 months between scans and 6 months since I should have had a scan. Sometimes I feel like stage 4 patients are left and forgotten about because I feel we are incurable so not worth as much time. The end of May 2023 I was once again told my cancer had continued to spread in my brain and it was a lot worse than my last results at this point I felt extremely let down by my team for falling through the net when it was time for scan results I was told I couldn't leave the hospital until I had been spoken to by a doctor I had to sit alone knowing it wasn't good news every thought crossed my head. And My scan showed that after being overdue for a scan I had 6 tumours in my brain the results showed out of 6 x2 out of 4 had completely gone after radiotherapy, x1 tumour had shrunk and the others that had previously been treated twice had grown 3 times bigger in 12 weeks after radiotherapy.

I was left for weeks knowing this news, scared and with no plan until one day I woke up with sudden symptoms, sudden loss of balance, unable to bend down , lay on my left , nausea and the room spinning meaning I was unable to do anything for myself I was given steroids straight away to help with symptom management. My previous scan showed that I had so much swelling on my brain that it had actually put that much pressure on my brain causing my brain to swell so much its ha d3 actually shifted in my skull.

Thankfully a few weeks later and a second opinion I was told my cancer hadn't actually grown x3 times the size like I was told it was actually something called necrosis which effectively is brain damage caused from the radiotherapy in the same area twice. We will be rescanning again in a few weeks by brain specialists, and I have been accepted for a new chemotherapy that will reach the blood brain barrier and hopefully finally stabilise the cancer in my brain for the first time in a year. My new chemotherapy would be starting in February 2024 I am really hoping this new chemotherapy is going to finally stabilise my brain the unfortunate thing is because I would be back on a chemotherapy for the first time in over a year I was aware this chemo was a bit harsher than my last and I would most probably lose my hair and Theo was now a bit older at 8 nearly 9 I felt it was the time to tell Theo the age appropriate truth I told him about mummies new medico that would make mummy feel a bit better at hospital every three weeks but mummy might lose her hair I am always careful to not say medicine to make me feel better as I know that isn't the final outcome.

A week after my second infusion of my new chemotherapy I had been up all night throwing up and I hadn't eat for days and I was unable to keep even water down I had been sick all night my partner rang 999 because of my history and I was acting irrational 999 said they didn't feel they needed to come out but the next day they rang me back and I spoke to them and felt fine, two hours later I was tired from being up all night and I went asleep for a nap it was about 1pm on 27th march 2024 and I don't remember but I woke up screaming and had my first two seizures my partner Liam rang 999 and my mum I had already had 2 seizures by the time my mum and ambulance arrived. I then went on to have three more seizures after each other. The sad thing is my son was off school and he saw me having a seizure while Liam was getting a neighbour and securing the dog in the kitchen while the ambulance came. The fact my 8-year-old saw me in that state is something I'll always feel awful for. It took two ambulances to be able to stabilise me enough to rush me to hospital and I don't remember the last few days of being in hospital I was conscious, but I don't remember anything really from that time.

As I write this chapter I have had 4 of my new chemotherapy sessions and I'm slowly recovering from my seizures and I have a scan due in another months' time to check my status of my cancer and I am praying for a miracle of either my brain to be stable or what would be even better if the tumours shrunk as in over a year I haven't been stable and I've had 9 brain tumours and because of the damage in my brain I am unable to have any more radiotherapy to my brain so I have to rely on my chemo options that reach my brain all I want is more time with my son.

Back in September 2021 I was meant to be a part of the original make 2nds count photoshoot which brought the original 20 girls together which was the start of our friendship and inspired us girls in creating our own charity fighting to be heard but unfortunately as I had only been diagnosed for a few months and I got scared as I hadn't met anyone else with secondary breast cancer and I ended up backing out of the shoot.

Thankfully I ended up meeting a few of the original girls at a make 2nds count retreat a few months after the shoot which is were we became friends and I was introduced to the rest of the girls and our friendship grew I always say I am the adopted add on to the group but they are the best thing to come out of the worst thing to happen to me I don't know where I'd be without their support through some of my worst times on this journey.

Setting up the charity fighting to be heard charity with the most inspirational woman I get to call friends and use our collective stories and experiences with primary and secondary cancer to use our voices and support those who feel alone on their journey and be able to help financially with our summer and winter grants is priceless and gives me a focus as I love helping others especially those in their early stages of a secondary diagnosis and with me being unable to work I know the financial aspect a cancer diagnosis can have along with mental health side of things I wasn't to use my time to help others.

I want to use my time and voice for change within the secondary breast cancer the lack of support for those with a stage 4 diagnosis, not having brain scans routinely and raising awareness for younger people my cancer was de novo upon diagnosis meaning it had already spread outside the breast to liver and bones upon diagnosis I was told on multiple occasions your too young. I also find the lack of being treated like an individual I feel oncologists don't realise the impact on our mental health with how we are told results or how long we must wait for the basic care we should be getting.

In Loving Memory

11.11.2024

FUCK
CANCER

"Live life for today as tomorrow isn't promised and appreciate the little things in life as when something like a stage 4 diagnosis happens it makes your realise what is important in life"

Katie Enell

CHAPTER 12

NIKKI WILLIAMS

May 8th, 2017, a day I'll never forget. The start of my journey or rollercoaster as some may say with Cancer. A few weeks earlier I had found a lump in my right breast. I had gone to the GP who told me to go away and basically stop playing with the lump and to return after my next period, which I did. I saw a different GP this time, they referred me to a two-week turnaround at the breast clinic.

I attended my appointment where they did a mammogram and ultrasound. During the scan I was given a needle biopsy there and then on the "suspect" lump. I was due to complete a night shift at the hospital and asked whether I'd be able to work. I was told that would be fine, so I continued with the procedure and was then ushered into another room where there were two ladies waiting to speak to me. My initial thoughts were that it was going to be a cyst, but I then realised quite quickly that it looked to be something more sinister as soon they mentioned the words breast cancer. Obviously, I hadn't been listening when one of the ladies had said, "you do understand what they're suggesting?"

And that is where my primary breast cancer journey began. The fear of that rollercoaster had emerged within me. If you have ever been on the Big One in Blackpool and that feeling you get when you're about to drop, I was there at this present moment of my diagnosis. Sickness, fear, anxiety and the threat of mortality was punching me right in my gut.

I had to wait another week before my appointment with the Breast surgeon. My partner and sister came with me for moral support. "I am sorry I have to tell you the biopsy has confirmed it is breast cancer." Everything else said after that was a blur! However, I do remember asking if I needed a full mastectomy and was reassured that it was an "insignificant find and that I only need a wide local excision (lumpectomy)". It's funny the things you recall. I continued to work until my surgery date, which was a couple of weeks later. I had the lumpectomy, radiotherapy and then commenced on Tamoxifen.

My goal before returning to work was to climb Snowdon which I did with all my family. It was a great achievement and still to this day I feel very proud of what I was still able to accomplish even though I was going through what was probably one of the worst times of my life.

Five months later, November 2017, I returned to work. Back into my full-time role as a Neonatal Nursing Sister on the Neonatal intensive care unit. I went back to work and back to the life I had prior to my surgery and was working 35 to 60 hours a week doing any overtime to try and fill up my pension pot and provide for my family.

Fast forward four years practically to the day, I had been off work since the 17th of March 2021 due to pain I'd been having in my back and around my right side under my ribs on and off for almost 2 years. The pains by now had ramped up and had become quite severe, the medications I had been prescribed were no longer relieving that pain. I was then given MRI scan on my back and was admitted to A&E.

By now it was 2nd May, I was glad I had finally had a scan to try and get to the bottom of my pain. Following that scan I didn't go home. I was asked to wait in the radiography department whilst a doctor reviewed my scan due to the amount of pain I was in.

A gentleman came to get me as he went to fetch a wheelchair; I told him it was fine as I'd already driven to the hospital and had walked to the scanner. He said it was policy and that he'd take me to A&E where I would get some results from the doctor. That's when I started to think something wasn't right.

I was wheeled round to A&E and then left there as he handed my details in to the receptionist. Obviously, I knew that this wasn't normal, to go straight from an MRI scan to the A&E department. I started to worry that something wasn't quite right.

I tried to phone home but couldn't get hold of anybody due to the signal in the hospital. Shortly after I was taken to A&E, I was called in to be triaged by a nurse. The nurse proceeded to check all my observations and then move me around to another cubicle behind the nursing triage station. Here I was given COVID swabs and MRSA swabs and had my bloods taken, I asked why they were doing all these investigations and the HCA who was attending to me said she would try and find out. A few minutes later she came back and said she didn't know; she'd just been asked to get these tests for a doctor.

Following this I was then taken around to a trolley in majors. I only know this because it was the same hospital that I was working in. After being put onto a trolley a doctor came in and put his hand on my shoulder, his words," I'm sorry to have to tell you, you've got a small lesion on your spine causing spinal cord compression."

At the time I didn't really take in what he was saying, I asked him, "Do you mean that one of my discs is pressing on my spine? Do I have a slipped disc?" to which he replied, "No you have a lesion," so I then asked, "What do you mean by a lesion? Do you mean I've got a tumour on my spine?" And he said, "Yes this is what is causing some spinal cord compression, so I am going to phone the Neuro and Spinal specialists as well as the cancer centre to discuss your options."

That's when my world came crashing down and I knew this wasn't good news. I started to cry; I also still hadn't been able to get hold of my family. The doctor gave me some tissues and apologised again and just said, "I'm so sorry, I'm so sorry."

I asked if I could try and phone somebody. "Yes of course, you can have a family member come in with you." At the time it was still COVID, so you weren't allowed to have people with you going to hospital appointments. Hence why I was there on my own. I eventually managed to get hold of my sister Andrea and tell her the news. Whilst telling her I felt immense guilt.

Only the year before we'd lost both parents to COVID 11 days apart. Our family had already gone through hell and back. Now, I felt like I was putting this burden onto them. They would now have to deal with my diagnosis, whatever that may be. Not long after I spoke to my sister, she managed to get hold of my partner John, and both met with me in A&E. As they arrived, the Doctor also came back with the news he had spoken to the consultants at the Walton Neuro

Hospital, who'd told him I was probably going to need surgery on my spine, and I'd need to lie flat on my back due to cord compression.

After being given all this devasting news I was then transferred to another part of the A&E department and John was able to stay with me although my sister had to go home. It was on arrival here that reality struck me when I asked if I could go to the toilet and was told, 'I'd have to use a bedpan due to the need of lying flat on the trolley, under no circumstances was I to sit up, not even to use the toilet.' I wasn't allowed to move myself or roll myself over, so had to rely on the nursing staff to log roll me onto a bedpan. By now it was Sunday night, and I was told I'd be transferred to the Walton Neuro Hospital by ambulance the following day.

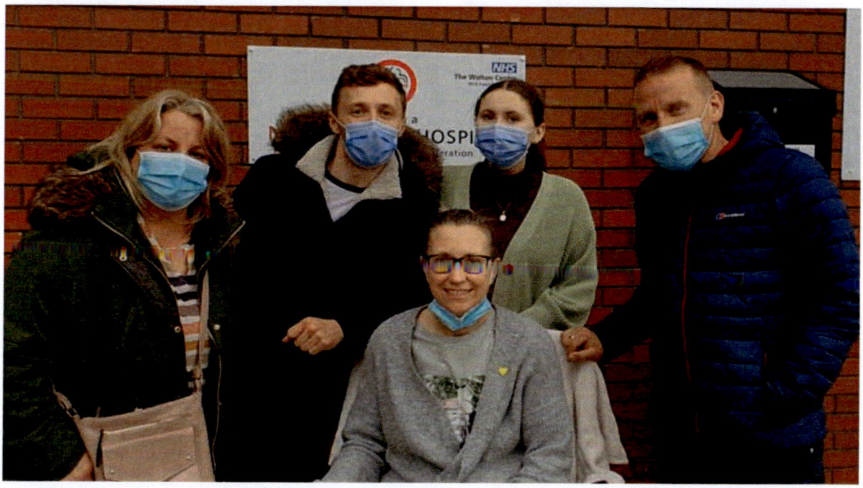

I asked the nurses if John and the children would be allowed to come in, because at this point I didn't know when I would get to see anybody again or what the surgery would involve, the surgery I was about to face would mean being put to sleep and any general anaesthetic comes with a risk, so I needed that reassurance of my family. I wanted to see the children before I was moved.

Monday came with me being blue lighted down the motorway to Walton Hospital where I received the most fantastic care you could wish for.

The next couple of days were a plethora of tests and scans. On 5th May I had my life saving spinal surgery. I had to have decompression and stabilisation surgery to my spine which has left me with two titanium rods and eight titanium screws now holding my spine up.

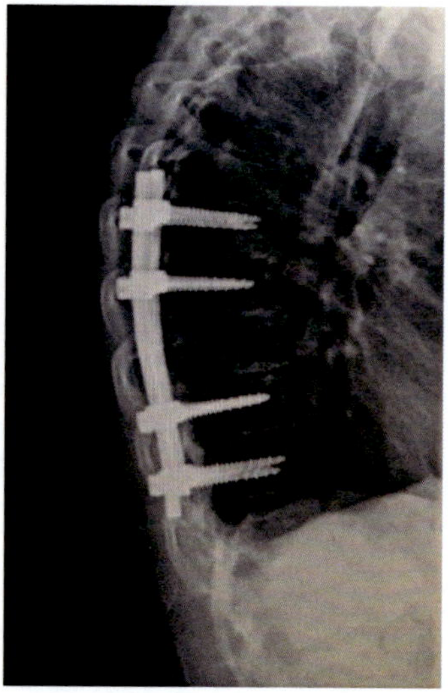

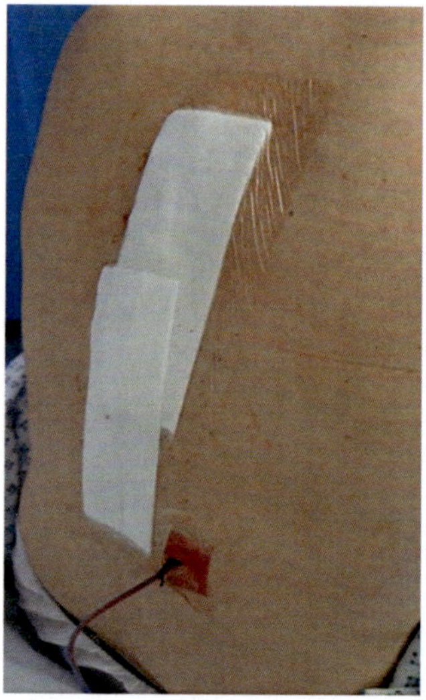

My Tumour was sent away to be biopsied, I was under no illusion at this point that it was cancer. On the 8th May I was being wheeled back to the ward after more post-surgery scans, where I met my surgeon, he told me the breast cancer had returned to my spine, that's where the rollercoaster became a little bit scary, that feeling in my gut I previously had was now a feeling of hanging upside down on the Big One.

Fast Forward a couple of months, I had met my oncologist, who explained I was now classed as "Incurable" due to my breast cancer cells taking up residence in my bones. I had Secondary Breast Cancer. (Advanced breast cancer)

I had radiotherapy and commenced on Endocrine therapy, Goserelin and Letrozole and Targeted Therapy Palbociclib and Denosumab, this was to continue until it no longer worked. This was now my new life. Four weekly blood tests, followed by treatment and three-monthly scans. I was aware of the life expectancy statistics, but I was also aware that these figures were out of date. I knew of a couple of ladies who had lived more than their ten-year diagnosis, and I aimed to do the same.

Whilst in hospital I started my own Instagram page @Spinalnikki to just document my new life living with Secondary breast cancer. It was here I found other girls also with secondary breast cancer (SBC).

Through the online SBC community I then came across Make 2nds Count, SBC charity funding research into SBC and offering support via online groups. Fast forward 3 months one of their posts was looking for "models" to participate in an SBC campaign for October Breast cancer awareness month, with nothing to lose I applied.

I was shocked when I received an email to say I was invited to attend for the project. All the participants were then added to a WhatsApp group set up by our fabulous Kate Orr. It was here we got to chat to each other, and swap Instagram handles to follow each other. It was then I first started to feel I "belonged".

Since my diagnosis, I had found it difficult for anyone to relate to what was going on in my head and physically. Now, I had a bunch of girls who all just "got it." One of those girls was Natalie. We discovered we lived in the same area and so we decided to travel together for the shoot.

The day of the shoot arrived. Natalie came to pick me up. Walking into that gym, we didn't know what to expect. It was fine! I got chatting to some of the other girls and we shared our diagnosis and treatments with each other. The gym was full of life, hustle and bustle. The one thing that stood out for me was how, you wouldn't be able to say that we had incurable cancer, everyone looked so beautiful! We were pampered and made to feel extra special by all the teams working with us that day. Vic and Marius from Sane seven were amazing!

As the day went on, I sort of attached myself to Kate as her friendliness, kindness, vibrance and "scouse" accent reminded me of my late Mother and Nan as they were both from Liverpool and it felt like family!

The Fighting to Be Heard campaign went nationwide! We were on billboards up and down the country, Me! On a billboard!!! It was a legacy for my family to be able to say I had helped to raise awareness of secondary breast cancer. I felt empowered by this and found my purpose again after coming to terms with not being able to return to my Nursing job that I loved.

We had our amazing F2BH girls as we all stayed in touch and a few of us even went on a SBC retreat ran by Make Seconds count, where we all met again! It was here I met Kate E, Laura S and Lisa F. I had followed Kate's story on Instagram, but we had never met in person, we instantly connected.

Kate E should have been on the campaign shoot but had declined as it wasn't common knowledge at the time about her diagnosis. We had both been diagnosed at roughly the same time, so we had that connection from the beginning. Kate, Laura and Lisa are now firmly in our F2BH group.

Sadly within 12 months of the campaign shoot we lost 5 of our girls, two of them never even got to see the campaign come to fruition, as they passed before the campaign was launched. It was at Sally's funeral a few of us that had attended wanted to do something more. We knew as a group we could not only raise awareness but that we could also help other SBC families too. A cancer diagnosis can be financially crippling. When you know you are on borrowed time, you want to be able to make lovely memories with your family but that also comes with costs attached too. A lot of patients lose their jobs as they are no longer able to mentally or physically continue to work.

We wanted to be able to fundraise for patients but for the full amount to go directly to the families. We even discussed writing a book to leave as a legacy to our families! So, in her determination to try and make a difference to our lives Kate O gathered a few of her friends and did a sponsored walk from Blackpool Tower to Radio City Tower to raise money for all the F2BH WhatsApp girl's families for Christmas, which she completed true to her word. My daughter and I joined them for the last leg towards Liverpool and the Tower.

From here the rest as they say is history!

This when Fighting to be Heard was actually born and where I started to live with Secondary Breast Cancer. I did not want to let it define me as a person. It had already taken away my health, my career and my future, I was now taking back control!

The friendships formed from F2BH girls coming together is the most significant and beautiful thing that Cancer has given me, it became my new purpose to support other Secondary breast cancer patients and families, also becoming one of the 20 Founders and trustees of F2BH Foundation Charity gave me a newfound reason to keep pushing. If it wasn't for cancer, I would not have met the most inspiring, courageous, determined, beautiful, kind and loving people who I now get to call my friends.

This disease is ever evolving and plays with your mind as well as your physical body, it causes you to have such dark moments, mainly late at night when we can "chat" to our fellow SBC girls who completely "get it" gives us that freedom to just be normal for a little while. As much as friends and family are supportive, they aren't the ones dealing with this diagnosis every waking moment. It can be hard for them to fully understand, that's why "Finding your tribe" like F2BH is so important.

I have been able to spend time with family, friends and F2BH girls. I might have lost my career, but I have had lots of experiences that I wouldn't have had otherwise.

I have appeared on billboards across the UK, been on TV and met some amazing people including my teen idol Peter Andre (who my Mum also adored!), attended Sophia Websters store Opening, dined at the Savoy, networked with other Breast cancer patients and charities. I even decided to buy myself a caravan with my pension, which I love and find it to be my place of quietness, relaxation and calm.

I have also been published in a collection of cancer stories in a book, created by Phil Alderson, "Someone's Survival Guide, Real Stories and advice from Breast Cancer survivors". I got to attend Ed Sheeran and Scouting For Girls concerts, Festivals, Charity functions and raised money for F2BH as well as my Cancer hospital.

The friends I have made through F2BH have become extended family. We have laughed and cried. Kate Orr has become a very close friend and confidante. She is my soul sister who I have shared so much with in these last 3 years, but it feels like we have known each other a lifetime! So as difficult as the diagnosis of cancer was, I am grateful to have met so many wonderful people who have played such a huge role on the journey I now find myself on.

Kate E is my Secondary daughter, we always joke about this! I introduced her to a local Liverpool support group, where she is the youngest member. Kate has been instrumental in fighting for brain scan's to be part of our scan check-ups.

We have travelled to London where I introduced her to a lady called Brogan. They became close as they both had suffered similar experiences. Sadly, we lost Brogan in October 2023. Kate O and I had been on a caravan trip and Brogan was also on the same site.

We walked together on Llandudno pier and Brogan and her daughter brought us pancakes in the morning courtesy of Brogans hubby. We had lots of giggles!!!

Then where do I begin with our Kate R. A phenomenal friend. Who despite her own diagnosis and difficulties threw a huge charity DJ gig in Manchester where we had the best night dancing and singing and just “being”, it was a night I won’t forget! Kate raised a fantastic amount for F2BH and continues to do so via friends. She inspires me as she is so focussed and driven. Introducing me to Indian tapas in her hometown, where we just talked and talked. Walking together up Moel Famau when Lisa J organised a F2BH charity walk, and her hubby Mark walking with me back down as I was the last person to descend! Taking me to her hubby’s Pub and just being a great friend not to mention a fabulous Trustee of our charity, working so hard behind the scenes! Kate is a truly exceptional person.

However, a huge thank you goes to my daughter Charlotte, my son Jamie, my Sister Andrea, brother Marc, John, Sophie and my best friend Debbie, for being right beside me riding this rollercoaster. Without them this ride would be even more turbulent.

Update from 2025.

Fast forward to June 2025. 29th to be exact. A day I never thought I would get to see.

I became a Nanna for the first time!

My gorgeous grand-daughter Delilah Valerie made her safe entrance into the world, thanks to Sophie an amazing Mummy! My Baby boy became a Daddy. Myself, Charlotte my daughter was there to greet her within her first hour. I feel immensely blessed that I am able to be a part of her life.

To top it all my sister also became a Nanna for the first time in August, Romie Seren was born to Chloe and Jordan, my great niece. Now our days consist of pram walks and lots of cuddles. Every day on this earth is a blessing and I now have even more of a fight to stay around for many years to watch our next generation grow.

This is why we need to continue Fighting to be heard, not just for ourselves but for our future generations.

CHAPTER 13

LISA JONES

I'd like to start my story by saying this is not a pity story. My journey has shaped me into the person I am today. Although the dream would be to live cancer free, that was never meant to be. My cancer story has allowed me to grow as a person, view life differently and has also given me a lot of wonderful opportunities. For that I will always be grateful.

I am Lisa Danielle Jones, 38 years old from North Wales. I am married to Rob Jones. And have 3 beautiful girls, Louisa 16, Sasha 15 and Aria 7. My family has been amazing throughout everything. They've accepted so much and have supported me every step of the way.

So rewind to where it all began. In November 2016 we saw the birth of our third and final daughter Aria. My initial cancer diagnosis came soon after her birth. My post pregnancy smear indicated cervical cancer. It was caught at stage 1 so we managed to get rid of it with a hysterectomy. Leaving my ovaries to save me hitting early menopause. So apart from a little sadness over losing my choice for more children. And a brief hiccup of sepsis. I escaped this episode of cancer without much effect on my life. I returned to work and put it all behind me.

In June 2018 exactly a year post surgery I started experiencing some pain in my breast. I feel it important to highlight this symptom. As everyone told me it won't be cancer. Cancer isn't painful. That is a myth.

My cancer only showed symptoms through pain. And I knew in my gut it was cancer. When I visited the GP they felt a lump so referred me to the breast clinic. A mammogram and biopsy confirmed it was cancer. We then had to determine if this was a new primary cancer. Or a secondary cervical cancer. It was in fact a new primary breast cancer. Unbeknown to me breast cancer isn't a one size fits all. There are different types, grades and stages. My cancer was determined as an aggressive form which is triple negative breast cancer. No clue what that meant I turned to Dr Google. If you ever find yourself in this position don't do that! Best get explanations from professionals as Google is often out of date. So what is triple negative breast cancer? Triple negative means the cancer cells don't have estrogen or progesterone receptors and neither do they make any of the her2 protein. Triple negative only accounts for 10 to 15% of all breast cancer. My treatment for this was surgery to remove the lump. Followed by 6 months of chemotherapy. I had a reaction to a type of chemotherapy which set us back a little. I also had a slight reaction to the dye they used during surgery. Which basically defines my story. If something is rare you can count on me being that small percentage who it will happen to. But we've learnt to laugh through these obstacles.

During my treatment my gynae team made the decision to test me for the brca gene. People who inherit a brca mutation are more likely to experience certain types of cancer. Of course I tested positive and this was to the brca 2 mutation. They tested me for brca 1 and 2. New mutations are always being discovered. Therefore anyone

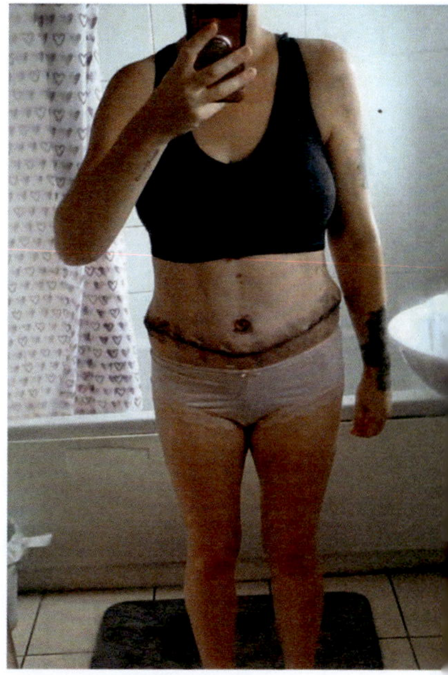

who has tested negative may test positive to something in the future. Self advocate if you feel you need testing. Push and push for anything you feel necessary. Having the brca mutation changed a few things in my journey so it was important to discover.

Following the discovery I underwent a bilateral mastectomy with an immediate diep flap reconstruction. This is where they used a flap from my stomach area to recreate the breasts instead of implants. The surgery was very long, 13 hrs. And the recovery was very tough. And even now 5 years later my surgeries haven't been completed. I've been waiting for the next surgery for 2 years now. I was initially told a 6 month wait. I know its trivial after everything.

I just feel my self confidence is at an all time low. The radiotherapy I went on to have has completely ruined 1 side and changed the way its heeled. After the breast surgery they also removed my ovaries. Which threw me into immediate menopause overnight. Again I had to self advocate to see a specialist who could help. As I couldn't have hrt, I was really struggling. GPs and so on don't really understand how to treat early menopause. Therefore it's so important you get seen by the right people who can help. Having the brca mutation had a huge effect on my family. It was inherited by 1 of my parents. So the 1st step was to find out which 1. It came from my dad. So once we discovered that my dad's family needed testing. We discovered 5 more family members have it. And the worst part for me is waiting to find out if my girls have it. They can't be tested until they're 18. My biggest hope is that I'm still around to support them during this time. And the massive benefit from discovering the brca mutation. Is the family members who also test positive will now be monitored. And have the option to undergo preventative surgeries when the time is right.

It was during the recovery from my oophorectomy surgery and during lockdown I discovered my next lump. In my armpit. Sadly the cancer had returned. And it had spread across my chest and clavicle lymph nodes. Which meant I was now incurable. The good news was I qualified for immunotherapy. To be able to receive this you must test positive for pdl1. If your tumor cells have pdl1 in them you can have immunotherapy. If not then you can't. Immunotherapy is still pretty new for my cancer. However the stories are very positive. The side effects are also very manageable. My treatment cocktail was weekly abraxane and fortnightly immunotherapy. Draining but manageable. Added at a later date was 15 consecutive rounds of radiotherapy. It all worked brilliantly. I had stable scans then eventually no evidence of disease results. Which basically means the cancer is asleep. Over time the immunotherapy and chemotherapy has taken its toll on my body. My liver function was up and down. And I suffer from peripheral neuropathy in my hands and feet. And to be honest I was generally exhausted. I have also developed an under active thyroid. The immunotherapy attacks everything in your body. So its over attacked my thyroid and ill be on medication for the rest of my life. It is very manageable so I'll take it over cancer. I also have fibromyalga caused by the treatment. Almost 2 years of continuous treatment had really battered my body. And mind to an extent. So I was given a break from chemotherapy. And as my results remained good I eventually stopped my immunotherapy as well. I proceeded to have 3 monthly scans and regular blood tests. And so far.... 18 months later my results remain positive. My cancer is still asleep. My oncologist is made up. I am the 1st person he's treated with this medication and the results couldnt be better. Apart from losing my hair from the chemotherapy i did manage the side effects really well. With treatment I was told that statistics gave me 25 months to live. And here I am 4 years later. I've just had another scan result of no evidence of disease. This means that the cancer isn't visible to the naked eye. I will never be cancer free, as the cancer cells have passed through my lymph nodes away from the primary site. However, this is the best possible result for someone with incurable cancer.

My life is going really well. I focus on manifesting positive results. And that's what gets me through. I'm now back at work part time. I exercise. I socialise. I've even joined a parents' street dance team. Alongside co-founding our amazing charity, I am living my life the best I can. And I'm forever grateful for this little miracle that seems to be happening to me. A really important part for me is when my cancer wakes up. I can return to my treatment plan. This is because my treatment didn't stop working. I chose to have a break. So I will remain on my 1st line of treatment. This is super important as I'm triple negative. Triple negative has less treatment options. Things like hormone blockers are no good as the cancer isn't fed by any hormones.

I live my life being as positive as I can. Without cancer, life would have been very different. But it hasn't been all bad. I've had several amazing opportunities. I have worked with and modelled for

Pretty Little Thing. This was through another cancer charity, Girl vs Cancer. We designed and modelled post-surgery-friendly underwear. This was a huge highlight of my life. And the most incredible experience. I've also modelled for Forever Unique for International Women's Day. I've featured on The Real Housewives of Cheshire whilst launching the Fighting to Be Heard Foundation. And between companies and charities, I've been invited to the most incredible events. I am absolutely blown away by some of the opportunities I've had.

Obviously, the most life-changing opportunity was the fighting to be heard campaign. This is where I met my community, my support network and some of the best friends a girl could wish for.

The day I walked into the shoot the room was filled with love. It was very overwhelming. I was comfortable instantly and was made to feel so special. The teams that came to support us were phenomenal. People giving up their time to support us. Giving us gifts. Makeovers. Prosecco. Lisa Fleming and Kathryn Orr worked tirelessly to make this campaign work. The aim was to campaign about secondary breast cancer being the forgotten form. We can't fight for our lives but we can fight to be heard. We want support. We want research. Options. We want the same care that people with primary cancer get. After all, it's secondary cancer that kills. So imagine having emotional support throughout your primary. Then, once you get your secondary diagnosis, that emotional support disappears. This is why I focus so heavily on finding a community to support you. We stood together, wrapping each other's hands in wraps. Ready to shout. Ready to fight. And ready to be heard. Sane Seven captured the moments beautifully.

Then, just to make it even more incredible. One of our founders, Kimberley, got us on billboards via Clear Channel across the UK. We were seen everywhere. We featured in magazines and people were talking about it everywhere. This is when we decided we had to go further with this. And we came up with the plan to start a charity. Not to fundraise for research. That's being done. But to help individuals and their families. There is a clear gap for this type of support so we wanted to fill it. Three f's. Friendship. Financial support and family support. We pride ourselves with the fundraising and grants we give out. Grants to help make memories. Or to help with bills. We also offer support via our support group on Facebook. And we welcome family and friends to join too. Its a lovely little support group.

I came home from the fighting to be heard shoot so uplifted. Feeling much more positive. Hearing other people's stories and seeing how they handle their journey. It just cuts deep. And makes you realize life isn't over. You don't have to stop living because of a diagnosis. My own story proves that. Obviously not all stories are positive. But as long as you are breathing you are present in life. I've learnt to say yes more. I've learnt that taking time for me is so important. Whenever I go away for an event with my girls. I come home with my mindset lifted and oozing happiness. I know others feel the same. And my husband often comments on how important my time with my girls is for my mental health.

Sure we've lost dear friends along the way. It cuts so deep when we lose someone from cancer. Sometimes it makes you want to take a step back. And that's OK too. We must follow what our mindset is telling us to do.

One of the main difficulties I've found since my secondary diagnosis is being able to communicate with my team. I spend so much time ringing around trying to speak to someone. During my primary diagnosis, I was given a McMillan nurse who I used as a point of contact. In Wales, you don't get allocated a secondary breast care nurse. Which is insane to me since it's a secondary cancer that ultimately costs your life. A few months ago my hospital listened, and appointed us a secondary breast care nurse. Luckily for me this was a nurse who had cared for me since day 1. She is amazing. Sadly, her funding was cut. After some patients kicking up a fuss, meetings with the health board, her funding extended. But only for 3 months. Further meetings and reviews have seen this funding extended now until March 2025. What comes after that we don't know. My focus now is to continue with our fight. Fight to be heard. Make them realise how important this nurse is to us. We need someone to call when we have problems. When we want to discuss side affects, new symptoms, when we need results and can't get hold of anyone. Because sadly that happens a lot with the amount of work load the NHS has. Also when we need someone to talk to. This is my main goal right now. I feel as patients we are always fighting for something. And I'm sure once this is resolved, I will have something else I'm shouting about and wanting to be heard. I love our little support network though. We all share stories of our own journeys and it soon makes you realise that no 2 hospitals operate in the same way. It's not the professional's fault at all. Their workload is crazy. The NHS is stretched beyond belief. However, this is our life now. Living with and navigating our new life with incurable cancer. We have to grieve the life we should be having. We at least deserve a more personal approach in supporting us.

CHAPTER 14

SUZANNE WILLIAMSON CAVANAGH AKA FLOSSY

Written By Brother Dean
So Suzanne...

I'd just once again like to thank the people who were by Suzanne's side over the past 3 years and moved mountains to help where possible: Mum and Dad, John and Kieran, Jodie and Chris, my wife Lorna, and Linda and Leanne. Our Suzanne's story has touched so many people and that has been evident this last week by the outpouring of love in posts on social media and messages from all over the world. Even messages from people who didn't know her personally. My wife's friend Danielle made a fantastic post last week where she talked about Suzanne's bravery and defiance during truly unimaginable circumstances, and that this was "So Suzanne". The day she was diagnosed she was already putting plans into action of what she could do - she got straight on to the cannabis oil with no hesitation – So Suzanne. How cute was Flossy when she was stoned? Three years of knockbacks and increasing bad news, did she wallow in it? No. Alongside her medical treatment she researched every type of non-medical treatment and remedy apricot kernels, Reiki, Alkaline water, Soursop leaves, Meditation and Mindfulness, colonics, the harmonic healing egg, the 7 immune ice cubes, affirmations... oh and dog dewormer if she had read somewhere that it had made a difference to someone, then she was going to try it – So Suzanne. The Pandemic wasn't going to stop her. Whilst some people were scared to leave their homes, Suzanne was out and about—multiple trips abroad, more than me, and I'm considered the traveller of the family! Even though the world was on lockdown, she still organised a wedding in Spain, and she was determined to go. In a huge middle finger to Covid, 120 people flew over to Spain, at a time of tests and passenger locator forms (Suzanne was also filling them out for other people), but she was so loved, and everyone who made the trip was treated to the wedding of the year. And of course, she had 2 weddings – So Suzanne.

Flossy was considerate of others. She left countless voice notes to her nearest and dearest to keep them updated, and she brightened up their day. She even supported others during their own difficult moments. Her podcast with Leanne was listened to all over the world on Spotify, and she got messages from people saying how this had helped them. She became an ambassador for Make Seconds Count, and she was very proud of this. There are billboards all over the country right now showcasing Flossy, standing strong. Soon, there will be an article in the Liverpool Echo about her story, and once again, she is promoting the charity. Flossy started a blog, and people were able to follow her story there. Others in similar positions contacted her for advice, and she helped them too – So Suzanne. Of course, there was a private struggle that we didn't see. John was her rock during these times, and I am so glad he was there for her when she would have a 'wobble' or a 'whinge', as she would describe it. She wanted to spare the feelings of her family and friends, and that was So Suzanne. The last few months and weeks really demonstrated her sheer determination. She had booked a holiday for John in Santorini for his 40th birthday gift and was fully intending to go. When that wasn't possible, she rang me up to book a surprise cottage weekend in Snowdonia for us all – So Suzanne. We all went to Chester a few weeks ago for a lovely weekend, and she had a great time, glass of wine in hand, a fantastic pink wig, and even went on a boat trip down the River Dee. Even just last week, she was looking forward to going for an Indian for John's birthday and planning the birthday decorations for the cottage in Snowdonia – So Suzanne. My sister was a warrior, and I was constantly amazed by her strength and positivity. The scale of what she was up against is hard to comprehend; however, she took it on. A common phrase we all used was "you've got this" and I believe, in her own way, with her fortitude, she was a winner. From now on her legacy will be - when you think of any acts of determination and bravery, just think that's "So Suzanne".

SUZANNE'S CANCER JOURNEY IN HER OWN WORDS

Joy, Elation and Utter Devastation! Living with Cancer! "Hola! I'm Suzanne a.k.a Flossy, and now known as Mrs Cavanagh, est 2021 (more on this later) and welcome to my blog. Nice to see you here! I am going to share the highs and lows of this rollercoaster I've been riding since 2019! Some bits might make you laugh, maybe cry, but the message is mainly to show that life can be amazing even when going through shite! Always wearing my positive pants even if they do fall down from time to time, I keep pulling them back up!

So let's start at the beginning, on 23rd April 2018 I visited the World Museum Liverpool with my folks to see the Terracotta Army. At this point I was 12 weeks pregnant and waiting on my first scan. On my return home I was bleeding and had to attend the Liverpool Women's Hospital where it was confirmed I had suffered a miscarriage. My heart was broken in two as I had already made so many plans for my baby. Afterwards the hospital gave our little one back to us as ashes, we spread those ashes in the baby garden at the hospital. We have a little purple locket in memory of our lil star. The utter devastation of the loss of my and our first child together, but also my folks' first grandchild. Weeks of tears followed blaming myself and wondering what I could have done differently but those answers never came. Following weekend, my brother Dean treated us to pizza and drinks which was certainly what we needed!

The following months were hard obviously! We went on a fun day out in August 2018 to Manley Mere & I fell off something because a child climbed up behind me and I continued to walk over! I returned home, the pain was too much, so I attended Whiston A&E, who took

X-rays but advised me to keep moving. Next day received a call to go back in & was advised I had fractured my tibia. So followed plaster, crutches & brace! So basically, my shit cycle started in 2018!

Then immense back pain started in March 2019, trips to the doctors they diagnosed as muscular pain. I had a tiny black Volkswagen Up! and what a struggle it was to get in and out of and actually drive as I couldn't bend, changing gears using two arms! Safety first! No painkillers would work whatsoever, sneezing pinched my back and I couldn't wear a bra anymore.

Further trip two weeks later and I mentioned that I'd had a positive pregnancy test and a change in my breast. You would expect that at this time but it only seemed to be the right breast which we thought might be an underdeveloped milk duct, but the doctor referred me over to the Breast Clinic on a three week referral. In the meantime, I attended the Liverpool Women's Hospital who confirmed there was no baby. Boo!! Anyways, onto the day of my appointment at the Breast Clinic which was 3rd May 2019, I had a biopsy, mammogram and scan. Surely there is a different way to examine your breast than a mammogram, squished and squashed to within an inch of its life! Ouch haha! Sporting a lovely hospital gown with all my belongings in a shopping basket! After getting dressed, they asked if anybody was with me and I said yes, my partner is outside. So I went to get John and we were taken into a cold room with just chairs and tables with a box of tissues...which is never a good sign! They said they were concerned but unsure as to what it may be and so they made me an appointment to attend the following Friday. After a week of apprehension, we arrived back at the clinic on the 10th May and we were told that I had breast cancer. My first thought was "am I going to die?" and "will I lose my hair?".

John grabbed me and I had plastic glasses on to cover my face and they nearly snapped (the things you remember) but as I still had back pain, I was advised that I would be booked in for scans over the next to weeks!

We spent the Saturday playing crazy golf and met up with my best friend Jodie and her husband Chris for food. We had a ball as we always do, forgetting about everything that was going on.

I had a bone density scan on 22nd May 2019, I had to be injected with dye and go missing for two hours first, so me and my dad (Tommy) ended up dressing up and laughing our heads off in the Victoria Gallery and Museum, you know, as you do!! I returned to the Clinic on 24th May 2019 where I was told I had Metastatic breast cancer. There would be a review into my bone scan. My sister-in-law Lorna was with me for this appointment as John was at a stag do in Benidorm (he said he wouldn't go, but I said I would get the same news whether he was by my side, or on the ale there).

I had an appointment the following Wednesday to attend Liverpool Women's Hospital to discuss removing my eggs, but they advised that I must start treatment straight away, so my dream of having children was shattered! I had to go and collect my medication from the pharmacy and I called John but I couldn't speak through the tears so Lorna took the call and I can only imagine how he felt with being so far away from me at the time.

I know he got really drunk and lost his ticket though!

Fast forward to 31st May 2019 & getting ready to go to the shops for the 1st time since diagnosis with my stepson Kieran & my phone goes & it's the spinal nurse Mark & he asked what I had been told so I said that my bone scan would be reviewed. He explained that I would need an operation on my back as my bones were crumbling. I went into the Royal Liverpool Hospital on 4th June 2019 & had L2, T6 & T8 vertebroplasty.

Anyway, we had a night away, booked for John's birthday and he said we could cancel, but my hair and makeup was booked and I WAS GOING! Hell, or high water! We had a fabulous night in Alderley Edge on the cocktails, you wouldn't think I'd had bad news I'd had but, oh did I sob when I woke up!

OPERATION ON BACK

In all the darkness, my curtain opens and who is there? Leanne is another of my best friends! She had just finished in a show at the Royal and sneaked in and came to see me. She left her dad Jimmy outside in the car waiting. She didn't want me having this op without seeing me. It was the best surprise after another tough day! Having to use a commode after the operation was the most daunting experience especially with my toilet fear! I also lost height after this so John was finally taller than me ha ha!

I commenced on Goserelin which I prefer to call Zoladex (biggest needle ever, which I've never looked at since John said, "Fucking size of that!" Letrozole, Palbociclib and Denosumab (for my bones) every four weeks.

People said for me to get paw print tattoos over the tiny scars but you would never know I had an operation as it was key hole, what a daft decision that would have been.

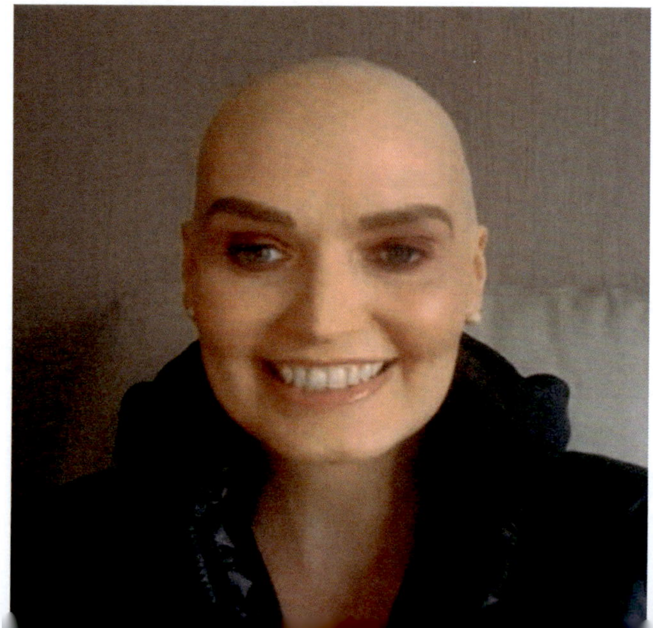

Absolute madness is this journey. After three weeks in hospital, I had the most fabulous curly blow on Friday 11th Feb. Fast forward to Wednesday and my hair has started to completely fall out. How I've sobbed. I'd have preferred to have lost my hair three years ago than now! I feel like I've lost my identity, but I know it's only hair. Wigs are brushed, a sequin turban has now arrived, so I've got this. Having a best friend who is a hairdresser is amazing! I'm collecting my hair in a Co Op 100% compostable bag haha! Sad that It can't be donated though. It is fab if I do say so myself.

OH THE GLAMOUR

23rd February 2022 Full on model photoshoot, oh my days! So! I'd voice noted Leanne the week before saying I'd love to do a shoot similar to what she had done for her 40th! In 20 minutes, everything was sorted!

Red Dress Arrived at M8 Studios, with Jodie, Leanne & Lorna with my dress bag & overnight bag full to the brim (not one to travel light). Only things I used from my bag were earrings & shoes. We met with Steve (the owner of the studio & photographer) & Meg (make-up artist). We had Percy Pigs, Maltesers & Chicken sensations (I couldn't get at these because of getting my make-up done). Skin looking flawless & wig in place. Dresses soon arrived from Cinders Party Dress UK, I was convinced they were not going to fit me but to my surprise they did. So helped into first dress by all 3 & the laughing we did! Changed into second dress, killer red dress with more natural poses. I felt like a million dollars!! Then we got our picture all together as these 3 are my left/right arm & leg, they get the tears & the ugly selfies.

We went to a coffee shop after the shoot and we realised we hadn't got a picture without my wig, so I said I'd do it there and then. So I whip my wig off and we are all giggling only to realise there was a job interview going on right next to us! A huge thanks to Steve, Meg and Cinders Party Dress UK. Also Leanne for organising and to all the girls for being there and having a ball all together! Hope you have enjoyed the glamour as much as we did!

Floss x

In Loving Memory

10.05.2022

CHAPTER 15

KIMBERLY NOBLE

Triple Negative, Stable and Positive

I live in Chester with my Husband Sean and son Charlie, I was born in Liverpool but moved to Ellesmere port when I was a young baby, I am one of 7 children born to our beautiful mum know to us as Dottie, life growing up was tough as mum was a single parent till I was around 10 years old when she met Steve. I went to Pool town junior followed by Whitby high school. Upon leaving school I trained to become a Hairdresser, which for most of my career has been in the Chester area. I have now been a Hairdresser for 30 years now which is a career I love; I even had my own salon in Chester for over 10 years till my secondary cancer diagnosis and sadly we had to close.

How my cancer journey started:

One night in July 2018 I was reading at bedtime to our beautiful son Charlie when he elbowed me in my chest, ouch I said touching the area, to my surprise I notice a lump in my right breast. I made an appointment to see the GP where I was examined by two of the doctors, both of which were happy it was nothing serious (so they thought) and off I went in the knowledge that I was in good health.

In August 2018 I walked down the aisle to Marry the love of my life Sean, little did we know what the next few months was about to throw our way and that I shared my special day with CANCER… we

went on our family moon and had such an amazing time.

Upon returning home, my breast did not feel right, I woke up with discomfort in my breast and under my armpit, so I made another appointment at the doctors where thankfully this time I was referred to breast care centre at the Countess of Chester hospital.

Monday 8th October 2018, I went with my mum to see the consultants, I underwent several tests which included mammogram, ultrasound, and a biopsy, I just remember hearing my mum in the waiting room asking the nurse if I was ok, I left that room and just cried I felt like someone had just invaded my space.

We went into see the consultant and was told she was 99.9% sure I had breast cancer but was to come back on Thursday for my biopsy results. I just remember the breast care nurse asking if I was ok, my head was screaming get me home I couldn't speak (it even upsets me now writing this) I remember being stood in the window when my husband arrived home on his bike, the bike was thrown to the floor because he could see how upset I was.

October 2018: I was diagnosed with symptomatic R Triple

Negative Breast cancer, my tumour was 5cm in my right breast.

Triple Negative does not have receptors making it harder to treat and more aggressive.

Triple Negative is more likely to recur and is common in younger people, black women and women who have BRCA1 mutation.

Triple Negative need more options of treatment and more research.

Thursday 11th October was a blur, thankfully my husband was with me , if I can offer one bit of advice it would be make sure you have someone with you and wait till you have seen your oncologist, they know more around your options, if your anything like me it all went over my head, thankfully Sean was able to listen to the oncologist, consultant and breast care nurses, all I remember was asking if I was going to lose my hair and Karen the Nurse saying yes Kimberly, your beautiful hair, but you have got this you will fight this, I couldn't of asked for a better team though they were super supportive.

Everything moved so quickly, lots of scans, CT, MRI, PET, appointments but I had a team of people fighting for me and I am truly
grateful to you all. Thank you to all at Breast care, Chester.

Karen: Breast care Nurse, everyone needs a Karen on their ward she made me feel so comfortable in an awkward situation. Love her, love them all Thank you.

Plan of treatment:

My first day at Clatterbridge Wirral, I remember us driving up and seeing the name cancer hospital, wow I was not at all prepared for this, it's like everyone there knew it was your first day, from crying walking in to feeling more reassured you have all these people supporting you.

Treatment for my primary breast cancer consisted of 12 x weekly rounds of Chemotherapy utilising Paclitaxel and then every 3 weeks Carboplatin.

This was meant to be followed by 4 rounds of Epirubicin Cyclo-phosphamide (EC for short) which is a stronger chemo, however I only managed 1 of these as I was hospitalised for 5 days having caught the flu, it was then agreed that I would take a break from Chemo and have my planned surgery.

Chemotherapy can only be described as brutal, it wipes you out, has horrible side effects and really makes you reliant on others. There are endless blood tests prior to treatment to ensure your body is well enough to take the chemo as it destroys your body's ability to fight infection.

During my first Chemo treatment, I tried using a cold cap, this is essentially a rugby head protection but with freezing cold fluid pumped through it which can hopefully prevent hair loss. This was really uncomfortable so I decided to forego for my future treatments. Losing my hair was like losing my identity and being a hairdresser with no hair was horrible. Thankfully, wigs nowadays are so so good, no one can tell if its real or not!

In March 2019 I underwent surgery which included Mastectomy and the removal of 4 lymph nodes, a biopsy of the lymph nodes revealed that cancer was visible in 2 of the nodes so a decision was made to carry out full axillary clearance as there would be a 50/50 chance of the cancer spreading if all the nodes were not removed.

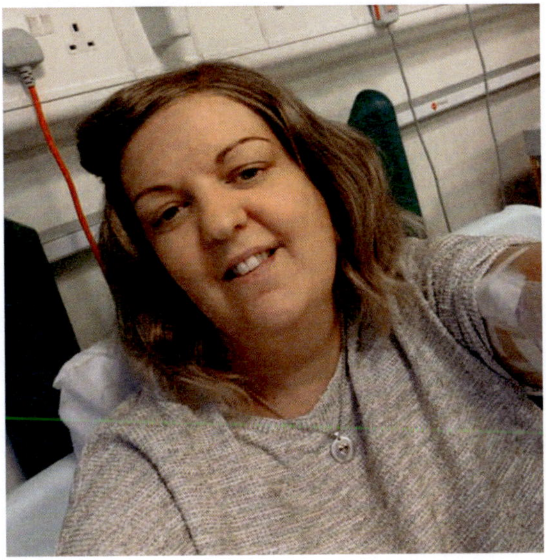

After recovering from surgery, I was to finish my chemo, on 2 occasions I required blood transfusions as my white blood count was very low, a big thank you to all those who donate their blood and time.

Once my body had a chance to recover a little from the Chemo and surgery in July 2019 my treatment concluded with 15 rounds of radiotherapy to the chest wall.

September 2019: I was given the all clear and the cancer was gone....

Even though I was going through treatments and surgery I still carried on running my salon, I couldn't of done it without Sean and my girls in the salon, Katie, Becky, Rachael & Hannah. We went through so many different emotions, Sean was not only a Husband, Daddy he at times became a carer and a Mum as the treatments were tough, sometimes I honestly think if it wasn't for my boys would I of given up, thankfully the blood transfusions helped.

While going through this our landlord at the salon decide it was time for him to sell the business and it was our time to buy, we went to see a financial adviser, My Mortgage Brokers in Hoole, Chester, and the planning started. We were excited for our new journey, unfortunately this was short lived as I noticed a lump in my neck and headed back to the doctors. I was referred to my consultants straight away and in February 2020 I found out that the cancer had returned. We decided at this point I could not carry on running a salon while on treatment and had to focus on my health so with a very heavy heart the salon closed in May 2020. Sometimes we wonder if we made a mistake but no it was the right thing to do at that time and meant we were under less stress.

My Mortgage Brookers were amazing refunding all our fees we had paid and sending us a huge bouquet with a message good luck with your treatment.

My new diagnosis was triple negative metastatic breast cancer in the lymph nodes on the left side of my neck, our world fell apart. I asked the consultant if this was going to in my words "take me" to which I was told unfortunately yes Kimberly, but when though we are unable to say. I went home not really knowing where to turn,

I broke down to my family, I wasn't ready to die, after a couple of weeks I released I had to fight this not only for me but my family, my son Charlie, I was treated with 15 rounds of radiotherapy. Radiotherapy was tough I got to round 12 and started to feel really poorly, I arrived for round 13 wearing a mask due to covid and was checked in, the lady on reception knew something was wrong just by looking at my eyes and I broke down I felt awful, I was admitted for the day, I was struggling to eat, sore mouth and throat, this is normal because my tumour was located at the side of throat, I was sent home with lots of medicine and thankfully had the weekend to rest, I went back on the Monday to finish my last two treatments. Thankfully this worked and the tumour disappeared. I still say to this day it was because of the way my oncologist (Dr Hall) asked for the treatment to be given, for the Machine to be moving while given my treatment, at the time Clatterbridge had said it was a first for them, but I am truly grateful for this.

I have been having 6 monthly CT scans and currently classed as stable.

Every day is a different day, I have struggled with neuropathic pain in my surgery side and currently under physio, I struggle with having my mastectomy as I feel people including my Husband look at me differently, I worry if I was to have reconstruction surgery, I would be putting my body through more stress to which the cancer could return.

I am now going through induced menopause due to cancer treatments, arthritis In my shoulder and struggle mentally because of the pain , I am a positive person and try not to show this but it is a struggle some days, I've lost so much since my diagnoses, we as a couple have lost so much not getting time just for us, people often say just ask if you need help but I am not one to ask, I've always been independent and probably always will be, I just shut the door after school drop offs and curl up in front of the tv.

Charlie is 8 now but was only 3 when I was diagnosed, it makes me very sad to think what Charlie has had to put up with since such a young age, watching mummy being very ill and having so many hospital appointments, yes, I blame myself but realise cancer isn't my fault it's no one's fault... Charlie makes us proud every single day even though he has his own (SEN) struggles (but that's his story to tell) just as this book was being start, he comes home from school asking "daddy can 5 of my friends come on Sunday" we are making a book, I swear I didn't even tell him about ours, thankfully one of his friends parents have stepped in to host, to Sean relief!!! every day I try to stay positive it's how I get through with the support of Sean, my sister Chelly and my best friend Sharon. Unfortunately, I lost my beautiful mum in July 2022 and stepdad January 2023, I could talk to mum about anything, that day I lost a bit of me however my sister Chelly the oldest member of our family stepped up and we got each other through each day, we were both close to mum and dad spending at least two days a week with them especially our mum, losing your mum is so so hard and upsets me everyday, giving me more fight for Charlie.

September 2021 was when I met the rest of the fighting to be heard ladies as I was invited to the first photo shoot over in Liverpool, I was very nervous but thankfully I have been a hairdresser for 30 years so know how to talk to people for the first times, it was quite an emotional day meeting so many ladies going through similar to you.

Meeting your people. People who get you and understand you I really could not put it into words, it's actually a thing, the group you don't want to be a part of yet once your there you feel the love and support.

I do have times when these group get me down and I just have to take a step back from them, seeing so many ladies struggling day to day is heartbreaking.

So so many ladies taken far to soon....

After meeting these ladies we wanted to get our word out and start our mission to raising awareness, we were encouraged to contact our local papers however whilst walking though Chester I noticed some digital boards so I looked up the company clear channel, sent the a email with a bit about our story, never thought much about it however I received a email back from them, I lovely gentlemen Glyn made contact and an advertising campaign worth £250,000 was offered free, our image first went live across the country in April 2022 and I am very proud of this, I am a believer in you don't ask you don't get.

We all met in Manchester and had a lovely night away staying at The Brooklyn Hotel, the hotel is amazing and have supported us on a few occasions, one of the occasions when we launched our Charity on the RHOC wow what an amazing opportunity, make up done, hair done, dressed to impress, we hit the run way at Menagerie in

Manchester I was a bag of nerves, I think we all were.

Standing up there telling a bit about my story and holding back the tears was tough, however I managed it.

We had the chance to meet some of the ladies of RHOC, so surreal absolute beautiful souls making us all feel so welcomed the support on the day was just amazing although am gutted I never got to meet Tanya lol.

How Kate pulled all this off wow, an absolute legend.

There is only myself and one other lady from fighting to be heard who have secondary Triple Negative breast cancer, I often get asked why I am not on treatment for secondary breast cancer? Triple Negative is like a house you have 3 keys (the receptors) however you cant get in, Triple Negative can only be treated if the cancer is visible, which is why my oncologist doesn't have me on any treatment, I trust her completely and I am currently classed as stable 4 years from my original secondary diagnosis, we need to raise more awareness, more awareness around secondaries and I really feel our charity can do this, we need to support each other because we get it, we get how hard the treatments are, we get the fatigue. I could not begin to tell you how many friends I've lost, how many people cross the street just so they don't have to speak.... I am still me, still the same Kim.

October 2023

I organised at Masquerade ball in Chester in aid of the fighting to be heard foundation, what a night we had it truly was a ball, I don't think most people sat down all night but I generally think that is because of our singer Rosalie, she was absolutely amazing... There was lots of laughter but also lots of tears the buzz around the room, from new people meeting new friends was just incredible and loads of sore heads the next day. The Night raised £2,646.00, I love raising money for charity as we do each year with our cake sales.

Thank you to all family, friends and neighbours for there continued support.

Thank you to my Medical team the work they do is just unreal.

Moving forward... honestly am not sure how anyone can move on from a cancer diagnoses, the appointments continue but you have to try and live each day taking tiny steps, having an 8 year old will keep you going, I try not to give cancer the time in my head as I feel we can all think the worse.

My only regret and one I tell everyone is get life and critical illness insurances, I never did and I never thought I'd get cancer at 40, the last 5 years have been tough financially for us. But the support from those around us has helped get us through.

Sean- Kim's husband.

When Kim first went to the doctors after finding the lump in her breast, we were gearing up for our wedding day which was fast approaching. To be told there was nothing to worry about was a giant relief as we didn't want anything to spoil our big day which we had been planning for nearly 2 years.

Roll on a few months when Kim went back to the GP's surgery as she felt pain in the same area I wasn't particularly worried, after all she was seen previously by two doctors who both thought there was nothing sinister going on. Thankfully, this time Kim who was seen by a different doctor was sent to the breast care centre to be checked out just to be on the safe side. If this hadn't of happened this chapter would possibly never of been written at all.

Since Kim was diagnosed with her cancer, it has been very draining both emotionally and physically for us both, all you can do though is stay as positive as you can and try to not let the cancer break you. As soon as you get dragged down by the cancer it is very difficult to pick yourself back up.

Life has been tough since October 2018. I try to keep myself to myself but worrying about your partners health, keeping a brave face on you, not letting your emotions show in front of a young child, taking time away from work all takes a toll on you. Luckily family, friends, neighbours and work have all been very supportive and without them life would have been a lot more difficult.

CHAPTER 16

LISA FLEMING

Friendships and Fortitude

As I sit down to write this chapter, I am reminded of the countless moments of pain, resilience, and hope that have shaped my experience over the last 8 years living with secondary breast cancer. Amidst the trials and tribulations, a fire ignites within me - a passion that grows brighter with each passing day. I have become resolute in my commitment to raise awareness of this disease that affects so many, to advocate for those whose voices often go unheard.

In 2021, as the founder of the charity Make 2nds Count, I found myself mapping out our awareness campaign for Breast Cancer Awareness Month. Teaming up with the force that is Kathryn Gordon, we turned to Instagram, gathering a remarkable group of women united by our diagnosis of secondary breast cancer, eager to amplify our voices through a campaign aptly named Fighting to be Heard. That day changed many of our lives for the better, bringing unity, support, and friendship into our often-isolating journeys.

Behind the image we captured that day lies a tapestry of stories, each unique and deeply personal. Mine began on May 29, 2017, when I was diagnosed with HER2 Positive, ER Positive secondary breast cancer. At that moment, I felt a deep confusion; I had never even heard of secondary breast cancer before. Life as I knew it came to a halt at the tender age of 33.

The weeks and months that followed were filled with hospital stays and uncertainty. During this time, I turned to writing. My blog posts, shared with family and friends on Facebook, became my armour and my support network. Each post reflected the strength and vulnerability intertwined within me.

Through the highs and the lows, the tears and triumphs, I unwittingly laid the foundations of my own story. As I began to map out this chapter, I found myself drawn back to those early posts that helped carry me through the darkest nights. They not only provided an outlet but also guided me toward finding joy in life again.

The Beginning of the Battle: July 9, 2017

This post is one I never thought I would write. Too many of my close friends and family were being asked questions, and it wasn't fair to put them in an awkward position any longer. So, no, I haven't vanished. Six weeks ago, my life changed forever when I was told I had secondary breast cancer. The words were surreal; I can't fully explain what it was like to hear. I had no visible lumps just massive amounts of pain attributed to a chronic condition I had lived with for 15 years. This pain turned out to be the 'bastard' that had spread to my bones. I didn't even know secondary or metastatic breast cancer existed.

If you Google it, you read the worst: yes, it's incurable, but it's treatable, and my team at the Spire Murrayfield is amazing. I've been hospitalized for almost three weeks, having undergone two large surgeries on my spine to remove collapsed vertebrae. I am now officially the bionic woman, complete with metal powers! Chemo and radiotherapy will follow in the next fortnight, and I'm ready to keep fighting.

Twenty-nine years ago, I spent my fifth birthday in the hospital after having a tumor removed from next to my kidney. Tomorrow, I will spend my 34th birthday in the hospital fighting this fight. Over the past six weeks, I have surrounded myself with my closest friends and family. An amazing group of people has shown their support in countless ways, understanding when I can't text back but still reaching out, cooking meals, sending little treats, and simply being there. I absolutely cannot do this without them.

I wish I could say I had the strength to be one of those women who take selfies of their journey, but right now, I don't. If this post can do anything, I want it to raise awareness. Tonight, when getting changed, whether you're female or male, take an extra couple of minutes to check yourself. Yes, it might feel weird, but if you notice anything, GET IT CHECKED!

Looking Back: December 31, 2017

As 2018 approaches, I'm uncertain how to feel. On paper, they said I wouldn't be here now. Life has felt like smoke and mirrors. Social media has been a good way for me to raise awareness of secondary breast cancer and the journey you embark on when diagnosed, but it can be hard to watch others continue with 'normal life' while we adapt to our 'new normal.' My family and I are so grateful for all the support we have received and hope to continue receiving on this journey.

So, where are we now? Thank goodness, chemo has finished! I will continue with three-weekly IV infusions of two strong drugs, along with my daily 'cocktail' to keep the pesky cancer at bay. In early December, we had a scare when a shadow appeared on my brain scan, necessitating a head operation to remove a remnant of it, along with another spinal operation and lumpectomy to kick off 2018. However, I am lucky enough to have enjoyed an amazing Christmas feeling great with my boys!

2017 may not hold many good memories, but it taught us that life is precious. Take the time to give your loved ones that extra squeeze, don't waste time arguing over trivial things, and don't be ashamed to reach out to those who support you. We can't guarantee health and happiness in 2018, but we can guarantee that we have an incredible support network (you know who you are) who has stepped up to the mark time and again. For that, I am so thankful.

As 2018 approaches, go get pissed, laugh, dance, and sing but most importantly, do those self-checks!

Celebrating Milestones: May 29, 2018 – FU Cancer, First Cancerversary

Thank you for all the support with the evening news article yesterday. It was hard to do, but for the right reasons. I couldn't read it in print until late last night; it felt surreal.

One year ago today, our lives changed forever. Being told I had breast cancer and then that it was secondary incurable breast cancer is a feeling I cannot put into words – a feeling I still battle with mentally and physically every day.

The hardest part of that day was telling my family and a small circle of close friends. It took me over a month to tell anyone else, and several months to see anyone outside that immediate support group. What has happened in the last year still seems unbelievable, even though it has happened to me: two emergency spinal operations, one spinal block, six months of aggressive IV chemotherapy, losing my hair, ongoing hormone-based therapy, learning to walk again, a lumpectomy with full node clearance, craniotomy, brain radiation, and starting new ongoing chemotherapy. And through it all, I'm still trying to be a mum, friend, and wife.

I couldn't keep being strong without Euan, who has become my carer while also being a husband and father, all while holding down his job. I'm in absolute awe of him every day. When I was diagnosed, a Macmillan nurse warned me to prepare for friendships to end as the 'novelty' of having a friend with cancer wore off, or people might decide they 'can't cope' with it. Sadly, she was right. But instead of dwelling on that, I focus on those who are still here the ones who text, visit, or simply 'like' an update and understand when I cancel or can't make it. We've even received meals on wheels from some special ladies. Yes, life goes on, but mine hasn't changed since that day last year. I still battle cancer every single day, and I've learned that I can't do it alone.

Some positives have emerged from this, though. I've spent precious time with special friends and loved ones, made new pals going through the same thing, and watched my boy grow into a brave and amazing little dude. Somehow, I've even started a charity! While we often question why this has happened, it is what it is, and together, we'll continue to fight.

Reflections and Resilience: May 29, 2019 – Second Cancerversary

Two years ago tonight, I kissed Cameron goodnight for the last time, unaware of the cancer that would rock our lives. I feel I could write a book documenting the past 24 months, but I can't look back; it's far too painful. People tell me how well I'm coping, but if they saw me now, lying here in the dark, trying to process my feelings through tears, they would see the other side. So why should I pretend tonight isn't hard?

If someone told me that in the last two years I'd undergone 11 surgeries, faced countless drugs, and danced with death, it would seem unimaginable. But that's our reality. How have I done it? Because I have no choice.

Yet, cancer has brought some positives, strange as it seems. I've met incredible people, seen life and others in a different light, and started something my family can be proud of in the future. So, happy second cancerversary, you little shit. You came to destroy me, but somehow, we're still going strong. Anyone who knows me knows I like a party, so cancer, be warned - I'll see you again next year!

Finding Strength: August 20, 2019 – Open Your Eyes

The last few days have been eye-opening in the best way! I attended a retreat focused on finding your 'inner warrior.' It's funny how sometimes it's easier to open up to a room of strangers than to those closest to you. Being asked to have friends describe me really pushed me out of my comfort zone. Many replies reflected a Lisa I once knew: 'confident,' 'ambitious,' 'determined' - traits that used to define me but now feel distant.

Today, I took a big step and gave cancer the middle finger by helping a friend with events! For the first time in years, I felt a flicker of my old self. There's fire in my belly; someone has seen me as more than just 'the C.' This journey has taught me that you can thrive with stage 4 cancer as long as people believe in you. Sometimes, you need to take a step back, give yourself some TLC, and refocus. My boys will always be my number one, but I'm ready to carve out time for myself that isn't defined by cancer.

To my fellow stage 4 ladies, if you're struggling, I hope this post gives you the confidence to take time for you and not be afraid to show how you truly feel, no matter how hard it may seem.

Navigating Parenthood: August 28, 2020 – Mummy, Will the Cancer Wake Up When You Burp?

The innocence of my cheeky eight-year-old, who has had to roll with the punches of having a mum with stage 4 cancer, is both heartwarming and heartbreaking. When I was diagnosed, I promised myself I would never lie to him. He was only four at the time, and now, at eight, the word 'cancer' has sadly become normal in our household.

Last night, as he lay fast asleep, I kissed him goodnight and whispered, "It's still asleep." Yes, that's right the bastard is still asleep.

Struggles Behind the Scenes: September 24, 2020 Opening Up

"You're so brave," "inspirational," "what a warrior," and "I don't know how you do it?" These kind comments have echoed throughout my journey, but deep down, they couldn't be further from my reality. How can I 'do it'? I don't have a choice. Behind the social media posts and fundraising efforts is a person - a mum, a wife, and a patient living with incurable secondary cancer who is scared.

I find it hard to engage with the press; body dysmorphia and anxiety take over. You might see a confident speaker on stage or a smiling face in a picture, but at home, I struggle to look at myself and often face tears and anxiety attacks. I used to be so confident and happy in my own skin, but cancer has stripped that away piece by piece.

Slowly, my body has adapted to the changes, and I've had to learn to accept and embrace my 'new normal.' In all honesty, I'm not there yet, and I don't think we ever truly will be.

Celebrating Survival: May 29, 2021 – Fourth Cancerversary

Four years ago tonight, I went to sleep for the last time without knowing cancer was about to rock our lives. Four years into this rollercoaster ride, when the prognosis was six months, today and tomorrow are always bittersweet as I can't help but reflect on it all.

That day is etched in my memory the last time I kissed Cameron goodnight without my heart sinking and the last time I felt truly 'me' and cancer-free. I could fill a book documenting the last 48 months, yet cancer has brought some unexpected positives: the chance to meet incredible people, see life differently, start something my family can be proud of, create memories, and help others living with this disease.

So, happy fourth cancerversary, you little shit. You came to destroy me, but we're still going strong. Anyone who knows me knows I like a party, so be warned, cancer—I'll see you again next year!

Wrestling with Social Media: August 7, 2021 – I Love You, I Love You Not

Social media is a double-edged sword in my life something I love and loathe in equal measure. It's like that old school friend who makes you feel amazing one moment and inadequate the next. The connectivity among the cancer community on Instagram is the part I love most; it's where I feel I belong, a place to document my days for my family to look back on.

Yet, there's a flip side. I've deleted my social pages off my phone several times when I felt myself spiraling into negativity focusing on the number of 'likes' and feeling inadequate when follower numbers don't grow. It's a pressure we don't need. Right now, I'm having a 'lovers tiff' with the Gram.

I started my page to document my experiences and meet others; there was no pressure to create content, and the term 'cancer influencer' didn't exist. To me, every patient who reaches out online or blogs is influential. It's a balancing act, and you must ensure you're getting from it what makes you happy. Don't feel guilty for going off-grid; I encourage you to spend at least one day a week where you put your phone down and pick your life up!

Celebrating Milestones: May 29, 2022 – Fifth Cancerversary

To that frightened girl who lay motionless in that hospital bed five years ago: my world was plunged into darkness as I received an incredible diagnosis of metastatic breast cancer a disease I didn't even know existed. Right then, I wanted life to end; I couldn't see a way through what lay ahead. Yet somehow, I did. That six-month prognosis has become five years.

There's no miracle coping technique or self-help blog that teaches you how to navigate this life. It's your inner strength a determination to live that guides you through even the darkest moments. How do

I do it? Like so many others living with metastatic disease because we have to.

Five years ago, I was told I had incurable cancer, but right now, in this moment, cancer doesn't have me. Over time, I've learned to take back control of my life. Yes, I'm on borrowed time, but tomorrow isn't a given for any of us. Slowly, after hitting rock bottom a few months back, I am learning to live again, finding new ways to navigate life, focusing on those who remain a constant and are worth our limited time and energy.

Rediscovering Joy: December 19, 2022 – All I Want for Christmas

This year, 'Lisa' is back.

Five-and-a-half years of constant chemo, blood tests, scans, and operations have consumed me, eating away at me both physically and mentally. This Christmas wasn't a given not because of cancer, as it has been stable, but because my mental health crashed down around me.

Nine months ago, I never believed I could make half the progress I have toward learning how to live again with this diagnosis. Accepting that life has changed doesn't mean you have to stop being you. Yes, it looks different now, but that's okay.

In facing these challenges, I've found so much joy and laughter in things I used to love. Statistically, I'm past my 'expiry date' as I head into my sixth year, but I'm starting to feel the best physically I have in years. Focusing on what makes me happy, I know my mental strength will catch up. For 5.5 years, I've written openly about the good, bad, ugly, and life-altering experiences of living with secondary breast cancer. I've connected with amazing people in the community, and my passion for educating others won't change.

I don't want secondary breast cancer to define me anymore, so you can find me @living_as_lisa. I feel a sense of elation writing this and thank you for being along for the ride.

Reflecting on Survival: May 29, 2023 – Sixth Cancerversary

Six f*ing years! May 29, 2017 life changed forever in the span of a day. The prognosis was six months. The cancer had made its way from the breast into every bone in my skeleton. My neck and spine were both broken, meaning the NHS team deemed it too dangerous to operate. Palliative chemo was the only option, with hopes of making it to Christmas.

I'm not a fan of the term 'fighter,' but in those first few years, that's what it felt like a hard, painful fight to stay alive. I was blessed to have, and still do, the most forward-thinking oncologist, Olga, who found a private neurosurgeon willing to take a chance. Two massive surgeries resulted in complications and some of the darkest times I've ever lived through, but eventually, I could start chemo that August.

Fast forward six years. It has tested both my personal strength and my family's strength to the physical and mental limit. Fourteen surgeries and a ton of chemo and radiation later, and I'm alive! In the midst of the darkness, we've found light. We've travelled to incredible places, made memories with friends and family, and learned what truly matters in life. We've been ghosted by some people, but we are blessed to be surrounded by an incredible tribe who has lifted us up when we didn't think we could keep going.

There's pride in knowing we've raised over a million pounds for secondary breast cancer research, support, and education.

Sharing my story has been emotional and draining, but I believe we've helped open the narrative about this disease in the UK.

So I guess this sums it up, as I said to Euan on that first day, shaking in my orange chemo chair: "Dear diary, f* you cancer I've still got living to do."

July 10, 2023 – F*, I Made 40!

We may be in a different time zone, but at 1:14 a.m. UK time, it happened. 40, baby! The big 40 is a huge milestone for all of us, but it's always been my goal to outlive the stats and reach this point.

Six years ago, I turned 34 as an inpatient in the hospital, recovering from major spine and neck surgery with cancer running rampant in my body. The nurses brought cake to my bed and sang to me, surrounded by family who all admitted they thought that birthday might be my last. I felt scared and empty that day. I made a promise with a friend that if I made it to 40, we'd have a 'F*, I Made 40' party to celebrate in style, and boy, did we do that last month with all our special people.

As it hit 1:14 a.m. at home, it was midday here in Vegas, so we started the celebration with cocktails in front of the breathtaking

Bellagio fountains. Did I cry? Yup, tears of utter happiness. Here's to the next chapter. It's not the version of the story I would have chosen, but I'm entering my fifth decade ready to embrace it, live life, and keep making memories. Physically, I feel stronger than I have in years, and mentally, I'm working hard with professionals to find coping mechanisms that allow us to live the best life we can.

So cheers to life! To proving the stats wrong and living life to the MAX! Even better, since we're eight hours behind, we get to celebrate properly tomorrow! Cheers to living!

Looking Forward: September 8, 2023 – My World

Six years ago, this wee face had just turned five, starting school with a mummy who couldn't be there for him. I always thought, "It's okay; he won't remember." Fast forward, and it's frightening how much he recalls from that time. He was surrounded by loved ones-grandparents and close friends but as his mum, I wasn't present in the way he needed.

In those early years, every day was meticulously planned to get me up and down the stairs to sit with him for an hour. I tried so hard not to miss things, donning my wig and game face, but it wasn't always possible. I needed to conserve the little energy I had to cope with aggressive treatments and constant surgeries. We tried to maintain a 'normal' life whatever that means. My diagnosis wasn't hidden from him, but we never actively discussed it much because he was too young.

This past year has been a real transition as we've watched him grow into a compassionate young man who constantly looks out for me. Our bond is unique; he knows when I need a hug, help with a task, or just someone to lie with on a 'stuck in bed' day. It's a sense of nurture and maturity that an 11-year-old shouldn't have, but it's also a huge positive; you couldn't ask for a kinder heart.

One of the things on my 'F* it' list was to see Cammy on stage with the company I grew up in, where I met some of my oldest friends. Our bond grows as we share something that allows us to switch off and lets me just be 'mum.' We talk about the scans I've had this week and the ones coming up; he admitted last week that he gets scared if he wakes up more. I was honest and said, "You know what, pal? I do too." We hugged, and I felt that extra squeeze. There's no right or wrong; you know them better than anyone.

A Journey of Gratitude: March 17, 2024

Two years ago tonight, it became too much. I opened my eyes, ashamed to find myself in resus, scared but determined to rebuild what was left, to fight for us. Battling the demons that tore me apart, I slowly found strength within a fire in my heart. A leap of faith, a goal set with my counsellor, led me to find joy in something I loved theatre. Embracing the stage, the lights, and the applause became my haven, my lifeline.

To the Showcase family, who welcomed me in with open hearts and plenty of gin, you provided a sanctuary where I could express myself and pretend we were all in glee! Laughter, friendship, and moments of crazy fun became my escape. Trust reevaluated, toxic ties and bullies were cut loose, surrounded by those who build you up, not abuse.

The pain often remains hidden behind the squares of 'the Gram,' but over time, the shame has begun to fade. Though healing is a slow process, supported by loved ones and old friends, love is sublime.

In that reflection, I see a girl who has come so far, longing to be free. I wanted to reflect on this second anniversary of surviving the darkness, rewriting my story. With hope in my heart and determination in my stride, I'm trying my best to seek help, continue rebuilding, and embrace a newfound pride. Seeking professional help has shown me that there's no shame in that. I'm working hard to erase the triggers where the hurt still sits.
Thank you, pals, for lifting me high, for seeing the strength within when I could only cry.

May 29, 2024 – Seventh Cancerversary

Somehow, here we are, still standing strong. Seven years since life changed forever; this shit show has been long! Living with secondary breast cancer is a life no one would choose to write. Life's plans, controlled by treatments, can be pretty damn sh*y.

I've endured a lumpectomy and clearance, removing the site of initial pain, and underwent bilateral oophorectomy taking away future family plans; the hardest choice made not in vain. Major spinal surgery at T12 left me bedridden for a month. Major neck surgery at C6 tested me physically to the max as the extent of what I was dealing with began to reveal itself.

Ninety cycles of Herceptin, my steadfast ally. Eighty-one cycles of Denosumab never asking why. Sixteen cycles of Paclitaxel, which was a fight. Fifty-four cycles of Capecitabine brought all the joyous menopausal sweats day and night. Thirty-five PHESGO; my body didn't like this one and decided not to cope, so back we went to IV touch wood, so far I can cope!

I've had two craniotomies, literally opening my mind, and three emergency smaller brain ops due to sepsis when the brain wounds wouldn't bind. Post-COVID, I underwent four further smaller spine and neck fixations; my resilience continues to grow. And just last week, I had neck fixations, surgery 16, and relief in each step.

Through it all, I've adopted a f* cancer attitude and determination. Despite the darkness, there's still been laughter and memories made. I've learned not to take life for granted and to do it our way. Using this position we find ourselves in to help others has been a guiding light. We've raised a few million by helping others in the breast cancer community shine bright.

People often wonder how we find the strength. It's not easy at times, but we've learned to surround ourselves with those who lift us, not relent. So today, it's a "7" from me. I'm determined to rebuild my strength and keep singing, dancing, and laughing through life. Here's to that "10."

June 14, 2025 – Always have Hope.

We did it. We took a monumental step by launching The House of Hope, Scotland's first wellbeing centre for those impacted by breast cancer and their families. This centre represents not just a physical space, but a sanctuary where individuals can find support, resources, and a sense of community in a way of life that often feels isolating. The vision behind The House of Hope is to create an environment where healing and hope intertwine, offering everything from emotional support to wellness programs designed to uplift and empower those navigating the challenges of breast cancer.

Now what next?

Ps FU CANCER

What needs to change: Access to life-saving treatments for secondary breast cancer should not be determined by where you live; it's a postcode lottery. We deserve more.

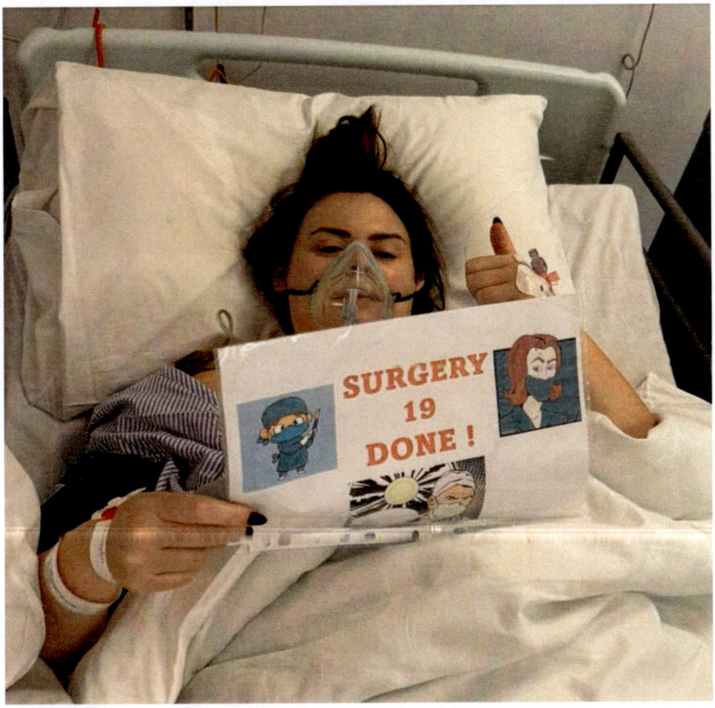

CHAPTER 17

OGE ONWUACHU

Keep Calm & Keep Moving On

My name is Oge, I am married with 3 grown kids, who will always be my babies! I am an FE college lecturer.

I was diagnosed with secondary breast cancer on the 31st December 2019. I have continued to work throughout my diagnosis and treatment, as it is part of my coping mechanism. This can be a bit of a struggle at times.

After undergoing various tests and scans it was confirmed that it had metastasised to my liver. I have so far undergone chemotherapy and immunotherapy. I am currently on a 3-weekly cycle of targeted therapy Phesgo® and I also have an infusion of Zometa every three months. I also take daily tablets.

So let's go back to the beginning!

In February 2019 I felt something was wrong, I felt a lump on my right breast. I wasn't really in any pain and was going about my usual daily business. I mentioned it to a friend and she advised me to have it checked out for my peace of mind which I promptly did.

I went to see my GP that February and she referred to hospital for investigation. This happened within one week of my visit. It was a bit daunting going to hospital for this. The doctor at the hospital examined me felt the lump and then sent me for an ultrasound. To my understanding now, they could have also sent me for a mammogram or even a biopsy at the time!

Once I had the ultra sound scan. The doctor had a look and dismissed it as an infection that would resolve itself. I was overcome with relief!

As you would think, the doctor can't be wrong!

Now I know better!

I thought everything was okay, little did I know, this was the beginning of a storm in teacup!

I keep wondering if I had been his wife, girlfriend, daughter, mother, sister, aunty .... Would his response have been the same? Could I have avoided being a secondary breast patient with no hope of being cured?? Only God knows now!!

'Oh My God, I'm Hourly paid'

My first words after confirming from the oncologist that I actually had cancer! You hear that one in two will contact cancer by the end of their life time. You kind never think it's going to be you. Well, I was that one this time.

Fast forward December 2019, still concerned, I went to my GP again. This time I insisted my GP send me to a different hospital. Once again, although she told me not worry I got an appointment in a about a week or so. On getting to hospital looking at my records, they questioned if a mammogram or biopsy had been done on my previous visit to hospital for the lump. To which I answered no.

It then dawned on me that I had been let down on my first visit to hospital for the lump in February!

I should not have been left to go home without a full investigation on the lump on my breast!

I had a scan, a mammogram on both breasts and a biopsy, all on the same day at this hospital, it took a while but it was all done on the day!

I got a phone call and a letter asking me to come to hospital for my results on 31st December 2019.

On New Year's Eve, with my sister by my side in the hospital waiting room, we watched consultants and nurses calling patients into the consultation rooms.

We laughed nervously, as you might when waiting to hear if you have cancer diagnosis or not!

Trying to lighten the mood we figured the nurses were sharing the positive news!

So we breathed a sigh of relief when the nurse called us. Oh no...
As we got in the room, our hearts sank when we saw the consultant's face. He delivered the news, dressed up in his bow tie,

in a very unemotional, matter-of-fact manner. Unfortunately, the lump on your breast is cancerous. I took a double take and said 'Pardon! What did you just say?' He repeated the devastating news.

My only response at the time, which I kept on repeating was, 'Oh my God, I'm hourly paid' I know, you think is that all you can think of… It was the shock talking, you think of cancer and you think my work life is over!

I was in a bit of a daze when I was examined again, the nurse tried to talk me through the procedures and the various tests and scans I would need to undergo, as part of the staging, to see what stage my cancer was at.

Closing Ranks

I had a bone scan, contrast dye scan, and MRI as part of the staging process. They wouldn't meet my eyes at one of the scans when I asked if they saw anything. I burst into tears and thought the worst. I was De Novo, meaning that it has already spread to other parts of the body. It had spread to my liver and there was a bit on my lymph nodes.

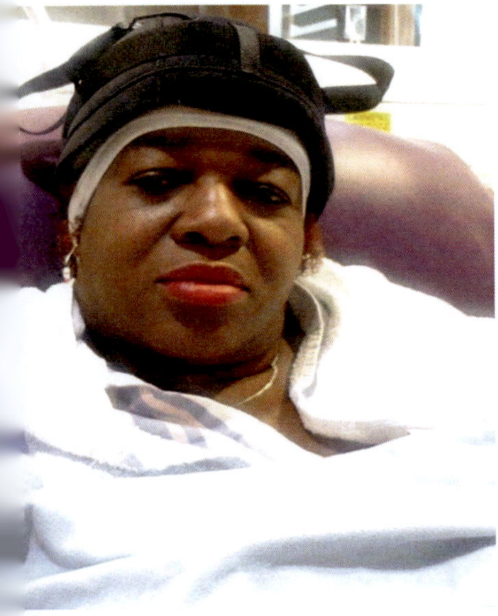

So, I asked the question: if the appropriate tests had been carried out in February, would the cancer have metastasised?

The silence was deadly, each I tried to enquire.

When they had done all the scans and tests and I was told it was incurable. I felt like I had been passed an immediate death sentence! I was asked to sign a document and tick in box that stated treating for quality of life rather the box that stated treating be cured, very daunting!

I asked the question, 'how long I had to live', fearing I'd be dead in less than a year. The oncologist told me to start the treatment that had been planned first and then it will be reassessed if it didn't work.

Advocate for Yourself!

I'm thriving with cancer, if there's such a thing! I don't really blame anyone, or can I?

No point or is there, too stressful! There's enough going as it is!

But, one thing I have learned on this journey (if it can be called that) is, looking for someone to blame wasn't going to get rid of it or change the diagnosis. It plays havoc with your mental health!

It is very, very imperative that you advocate for yourself!

If you feel that there is something wrong keep pushing!

Do not be fobbed off!

It's your body you know it better than anyone else!

Keep fighting till you are heard!

"Keep Calm and Keep Moving On"

I needed to concentrate on moving forward and tackling the diagnosis with as positive mindset as possible. Friends always share how upbeat I am. At times, I do feel sorry for myself, I switch off from text messages, work can feel relentless at times, it's all behind closed doors, as teacher my students are unaware of my condition which sometimes is a challenge, but I prefer it that way. I just say to myself come on 'Oge' pull yourself together, and try and shake myself out of it as life is too short. This can be hard though because it's always at the back of your mind.

Weekly chemo began just as COVID hit. Having treatment during this time was lonely, marking the start of my independent cancer journey.

For the past four years, I've been on the same line of chemo treatment with slight alterations. The worst side effects are neuropathy and fatigue, especially as I still work full-time. My feet are swollen, and I can barely feel them. I can just about walk at times.

It was a lonely world, and I was getting depressed until one day on GMTV, I saw Leanne from Black Women Rising. Reaching out and starting monthly Zoom calls with the group was a turning point for me on this 'journey'. As I mentioned earlier working throughout my diagnosis has been part of my coping mechanism.

I was invited to the launch of 'Fighting to be Heard' in March 2023! Boy that was another major turning point for me on this 'journey'!

I skived off work (best decision ever) and went down to

Manchester met these inspiring ladies who immediately made me feel so welcome, we clicked off immediately! The connection was and still is amazing and they understood the ups and downs of what I'm going through. Reminds me of the song 'We have something in common' I feel privileged to be a part of this charity and vow to support and be a part of it in any way I can. It can be hard at times because of the inevitable losses along the way. I think it is worth it in the end! The sacrifice, love support and support these amazing ladies show

This 'journey' has taught me to speak up. I used to bend backward for people, asking "how high" when told to jump. My tolerance for those taking advantage of my good nature is now non-existent. This strength has come from within. The little irrelevant things that used to matter to me before, don't anymore! Don't sweat the small stuff! My perspective on life is much clearer. I spend time with people I want to be with and do things I want to do!

I am immensely relieved that my children are old enough to look after themselves, though they will always be my babies! I count myself lucky on this believe it or not. It's incredibly hard to become friends with ladies who have younger children and witness them lose their lives while still being mums. The thought of their children growing up without their mother's presence is heart breaking, and it adds another layer of pain to this journey.

Even though there's no time for regrets, I would encourage young people, especially freelancers like myself, to consider taking out critical illness and life insurance. The diagnosis is unbearable, and adding financial worries on top of that can be just as difficult. If I didn't have my husband's support, it would be even more challenging.

In hindsight, this is why the financial and emotional support from Fighting to be Heard means so much to people on this 'journey'. You lose a lot financially and emotionally, you have the numerous hospital appointments which can take forever, having to give up work or hobbies due to side effects. It's a whole forced lifestyle change to what you may be used to.

I am frustrated that those who shout the loudest get the best treatment. It should not be so! If you're unable to advocate for yourself, you're often brushed off and made to feel like you are being a bother. It needs to be remembered we are not just a number. We are fighting to be heard.

One of my biggest positives on this 'journey' is meeting the ladies.
I know I am not alone!
We will Keep Fighting To Be Heard!!

NEVER
ACCEPT

CHAPTER 18

JEANNIE AMBROSE

Chasing Peace

Growing up, cancer was never on my radar, it was something that other people died from, not my family, not me. Youth and the blissful unknown, what a beautiful thing. Then, when I was 24, my Dad died from Bowel Cancer. He'd had it for 4 years and hadn't told us, not even my Mum. We knew he had been very ill, but he told us it was Polyps, he had an operation to remove 'them' and that it was just a matter of finding the right medication for him to improve. It was a nurse, who was arranging for a special mattress to be delivered to us, who unwittingly told my Mum. Dad said he didn't know how to tell us, and he died 11 days later. I often wonder what was his reasoning, did he not know how to tell us, or not want to, protecting us, or just wanted everything to remain the same? He carried it alone for all that time. What a weight.

It was a massive shock and a wakeup call. Cancer could affect anyone, at any time. My Dad was gone, and we were all devastated. My Mum was never really the same again. Then 12 years later, Mum became ill very quickly and was diagnosed with Pancreatic Cancer that had spread. She passed away when I was 37. I'm not one for 'why me', that self-pity would just spiral for me, so I don't go there. I wouldn't say I was angry, but I did feel a bit like 'hang on, I've been here already, done that, got the t-shirt'. But cancer doesn't give a shit. It doesn't care what the tally is.

My mother-in-law had also passed away the same year. It was a lot. My husband and I just hunkered down and focused on our children, who were then age 7 and 4. Reuben and the kids, that little bubble of family love, the 4 of us, it carried us through. My brother, sister and I, I suppose we all thought 'well which one of us will be next'. You can't help but think that in the back of your mind. Nowadays some would say I manifested the cancer happening, that's not my belief, and that kind of projection can be very damaging to cancer patients who are already dealing with the trauma of their diagnosis and are desperately trying to cope with it.

So, I started regularly checking myself. But vigilance didn't help me. My breast tissue was quite dense and I had tumours growing in both breasts. I examined myself, and as both sides were the same, I just put it down to me approaching menopause and my breast tissue changing accordingly. There was no stand out lump, just what I would describe as thicker areas. So there I was, merrily checking myself thinking I was safe. It was when I went to the doctors for what I thought was an insect bite (I'd been gardening and figured something had got down my top) when they suggested they examine me. He said 'how long have you had these lumps?' and my heart sank. He referred me to the Breast Unit at Addenbrookes Hospital and that's where it all began.

At the breast unit they told me that they were worried by what they had seen, I had 5 biopsies taken and was booked for a CT scan. The biopsies confirmed breast cancer. On CT scan results day the Dr said 'the scan has shown several things' and I knew it was bad. I was diagnosed with Secondary Breast Cancer in May 2019 age 47 with spread to my spine, ribs, sternum and pelvis. My lovely life with my husband and kids was totally turned on its head. I'd brought devastation into our home. Before she'd even stopped talking I thought to myself I've got 9 months. Where the hell did I pluck that from? Probably from the rapid decline that Mum and Dad had both had. So, when she said people can live with this for years (3-5 average) it felt like a bonus. Obviously I was devastated but just so happy to be alive, I walked out of the hospital, it was a gorgeous sunny day and I felt peace. I don't know why but I thought 'I'm going to be ok'. Not ok as in cured, but thank God that day my mindset was I'm going to keep living for as long as I possibly can. I will cope.

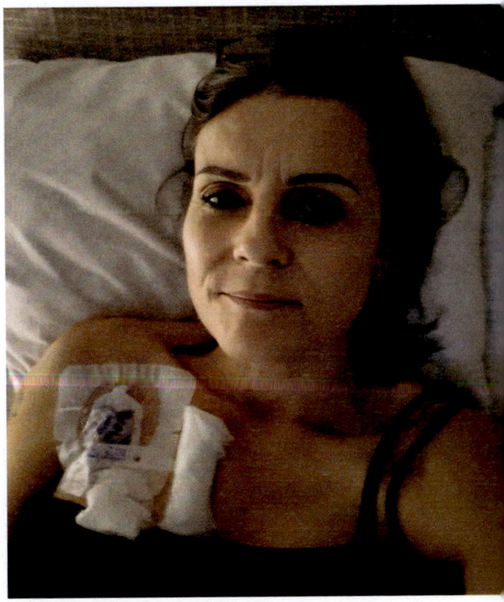

My cancer is Her2 negative, and we went ahead with targeted and hormone therapy treatment of Ribociclib, Letrozole tablets and Denosumab injections. I also had my ovaries removed as my tumours are oestrogen fed. My body aches and I have menopausal symptoms and fatigue but generally I was able to live quite well. I continued to work as a Surveyor for Local Authority Building Control. Mentally this is such a lot to carry. My children were 17 and 15 when I was diagnosed and living as normally as possible really helped us all.

I was offered by Addenbrookes Hospital to take part in their 'Personalised Breast Cancer Programme'. This tests your genetic makeup and can help them learn about cancer as well as possibly helping treat my specific disease in the future. The testing showed up that I carry the ATM gene, which means that I was at a moderately increased risk of getting breast cancer. It also meant that there is a 50/50 chance of my children inheriting the gene. That has been hard to deal with. The thought that I may have passed this increased risk on to them. We have discussed this together and they will decide if and when they would like to be tested.

Finding other patients in the same situation has been invaluable for me. When someone else knows exactly how you are feeling it's really comforting, it's a different type of support that your family and friends just cannot give. I'd had a little contact with cancer patients via social media but not much. In March 2020, 10 months after my diagnosis, the national covid lockdown meant I spent much more time online. I found opportunities to do things that I never would have before, I wrote a magazine article for cancer patients and did a charity skydive when restrictions allowed.

Through Instagram I found @seconday.sisters who, through their raising awareness posts, connected me to @make2ndscount. Lisa Fleming is the brilliant founder of Make2ndscount, and I began following her events and her campaigning. In 2021, she put a call out for secondary breast cancer patients to be involved in a campaign called 'Fighting to be Heard'. I'd never met up with a group of patients before and I was so happy to be involved. It was the start.

I travelled to Liverpool and met up with another patient taking part, Lesley. Instantly she was chatting and totally put me at ease. We walked to the gym where the shoot was taking place. I felt physically sick just before we walked in, I'm a confident person but the thought of meeting 20 other stage 4 patients, all strangers was exciting and nerve wracking at the same time. The first person I remember was Flossy (Suzanne). We were all getting changed and she was bubbly and laughing and I knew the day was going to be special. Lisa was beaming, she'd worked incredibly hard to make this happen and she introduced us all to Kate Gordon Orr. Kate was flying around organizing us all. Kate has a beautiful warmth about her, the woman is a powerhouse but is also incredibly caring and kind all at the same time.

As everyone arrived we were whisked off to different areas to have our hair and make up done. It really was a lovely atmosphere and I loved being pampered. We were all wearing black with our hands bandaged, boxing style, to represent Fighting to be Heard.
We were very lucky to be photographed by world renowned photographer Sane Seven. We were all stood in position and she moved us around to get the shot exactly right. Sometimes a subtle change but everything done for the maximum impact. I felt a solidarity between us. We are different ages, different personalities, yet this same diagnosis drawing us all here. All standing together living with a disease that weighs so heavily. I remember Lisa being protective, saying 'the ladies are going to be feeling uncomfortable standing for so long'. And that's the thing, we all looked normal and healthy but all of us are actually very ill.

For me, the moment that shot was taken was so emotional. All stood side by side. From the noise and chaos before, it was now silent in the room. The shutter was going and she was shouting 'one more, one more' and then finally 'we're done'. We saw the image and knew we had done something powerful. Tears and then laughter. I'll never forget how that moment felt.

So then we all go back to our everyday lives. It had been a wonderful experience for me. But then the losses came, 5 ladies within a year, Emily, Flossy, Cathy, Vicky and Sally. It was very hard to cope with. The reality of this disease is that you can find and make some wonderful friendships with other secondary patients. You have an understanding, a love and strength between you, yet one day, and probably soon, one will have to say goodbye to the other. Its very sad, you feel their loss and also it's a reminder of your own mortality.

Cancer has made me bold, made me want to feel more, experience more. To enjoy the mundane as well as the exciting. I had been diagnosed 3 years and I had the average life expectancy of 3-5 years ringing in my ears. My husband and I decided to by a van and convert it to a campervan. We did it ourselves, things went wrong, trial and error and eventually we had a workable van. We did a two month trip around Europe in our little van. The hospital were excellent, they gave me all my drugs for the trip and waved me off. My workplace were also very supportive, I unashamedly used the cancer card to get the time off. We covered 5015 miles through 11countries.

The kids flew out to join us twice during the trip, it was wonderful and I know we would not have done it without my diagnosis to spur us on.

I had carried on working and I had just spent 4 years getting qualified and gaining my CIOB Chartered Membership. Although as time went on I knew that I was too unwell to continue my job as a Surveyor. I have multiple bone metastases along with osteoarthritis, and one day, up a three story ladder, I had pains and thought I really shouldn't be doing this. I'd already started to feel really tired and unwell and considered handing in my notice there and then. Thank God I didn't, I actually kind of stumbled on the fact after some late night googling (dangerous but in this case helpful) that as a stage 4 patient I may be entitled to my work pension through ill health retirement. I had 2 separate assessments to confirm I qualified and it's really helped. I loved my job but I knew when enough was enough and retirement, I absolutely love it. Time for me now.

One piece of advice, if you are a relatively well person, think about getting critical illness cover. We had it for a while, then moved house and decided we couldn't afford it. Then 2 years before I was diagnosed, I said we really should get it again. It was a squeeze financially but I'm so thankful we made that decision. It made a huge difference when it paid out and the financial strain was lessened.

I'm amazed at the lack of help available to cancer patients in regard to financial options available and where to even start. Macmillan were a good place to begin but still didn't give me all the info I needed that was relevant to me. I'd never claimed anything up to this point so had no idea. Personal Independence Payments (PIP) were a nightmare to get, my GP helped but my mental health took a kicking trying to get it sorted. Persistence was key here, and appealing when they refused. I'm also entitled to a small amount of

Employment Support Allowance (ESA) which again I didn't find out until later. So as a family thankfully we are ok but its taken a lot of info gathering and chasing. The last thing patients need is financial worries which it can cause so much strain and have a detrimental impact on physical and mental health.

It was then proposed by some of the ladies to launch a charity to help with financial issues and friendship. We are all founders of the charity but I definitely cannot be credited for any of the work that went into setting this all up. There were individuals who worked tirelessly to get it up and running and I'm so thankful to them. We had our charity launch in Manchester, and thanks to Seema Malhotra, we appeared on The Real Housewives of Cheshire. Again, we were totally pampered, were gifted new clothes from Forever Unique, strutted our stuff on the catwalk and shared our stories. Emotional yet full of joy. Another brilliant day all together for Fighting to be Heard.

When talking about my cancer I personally don't like the 'fighting' and 'battling' words used. I don't want to think of my body as battling. I'm living and enjoying my life in the best way that I can. A battle indicates there will be a loser and that's just not how I want to look at it. But for sure it is a fight to be heard. At the time of the original campaign it was estimated that there were 35,000+ patients living with secondary breast cancer (at the time we had never been counted). Today we know that the figure is 57,000+ patients with 11000+ dying every year, that's approximately 31 a day (Breast Cancer Now). The funding that goes to secondary breast cancer research is only a very small percentage of all breast cancer funding even though secondary is the only breast cancer that kills.

We have also found that there can be differences in treatment pathways, availability and support depending on where you live. There are often cross border disparities. At the moment I am taking part in a campaign which aims to ensure that NICE (the body that approves drugs for use in the NHS in England) will approve the drug Enhertu for Her2low secondary (metastatic) breast cancer patients. Enhertu is a drug that has been applauded by the medical community and extends the lives of patients by around one third. It can give patients a good quality of life and many extra months with those they love. The drug is approved for use in the NHS in Scotland, 15 other European countries and is also used worldwide.

The problem that we are facing is that NICE introduced a revised evaluation system for diseases and introduced a 'severity modifier'. This new system now does not recognise metastatic breast cancer as the severest category which blocks access to the level of funding it once had. Before this system change in 2022, the disease was considered the highest severity and would have been approved. Now however, NICE have said that it is now not cost effective and will not approve the drug. I have taken part in sharing my story, signed open letters to government, attended an All Party Parliamentary Group Meeting arranged by Breast Cancer Now along with other patients and demonstrated topless at Parliament Square.

There are many individuals, patients and organisations all fighting for access to this drug and putting pressure on NICE to review the severity modifier system. If it isn't changed then ALL new drugs for metastatic breast cancer may struggle to be approved for use via the NHS in England.

At the time of writing NICE still have not made a formal decision on Enhertu for Her2low patients and their guideline advice is not to approve. This is despite agreement from many sides that the severity modifier is incorrect, (as per Health and Social Care Select Committee public evidence session 8th May 2024), NICE will not recognise that they have got this wrong. It is such a serious concern for patients and future survival rates and I have had my eyes opened on how unjust our systems can sometimes be.

I also feel that another area that would really help is prevention and early detection. Breast screening should be done earlier, mammograms at age 50 were no use to me and the strain on the NHS, my experiences in A&E in particular, have not been great. However, my Oncologist and team at Addenbrookes Hospital Cambridge are brilliant and have been very supportive.

I feel listened to, and they consider every question or suggestion that I bring to the table. Social media and other patients have given me a lot of useful info, I might hear about a different treatment, therapy or trial and I can ask questions about these. Be your own patient advocate, be pushy if you have to. My attitude is that ultimately it won't save my life but it could just give me some extra time.

So, for me, the fight is not with the cancer, it's with the system, the powers that be, the right to life and how to keep moving forward. Making memories. Fighting to be Heard.

I recently had the news that my cancer had spread to my liver, so a change of treatment for me and the mental challenge that goes alongside it. I feel that after almost 5 years diagnosed I can often feel a bit emotionally tired out, a bit jaded. But I have learnt a lot about myself. I now know that I can cope with more than I ever thought I could. I know what I'm made of. It's taught me how to live.

There will be incredibly dark days but I will forever continue to chase that initial feeling of peace that I had at diagnosis. I mean you could argue it was shock but I'm going with peace. Chasing peace, that's a paradox in itself. Like living with this disease, a double edged sword, I am incredibly sad but incredibly grateful all at the same time. Trying to live happily while knowing you are dying. That's the trick. Finding peace and maintaining a happy life for myself and for my family.

CHAPTER 19

ROISIN PELAN

The Beginning I Never Asked For

I look back at that person now and I just want to scoop her up and tell her there is so much hope and light and joy to come. I was 32 when I was first diagnosed. I'd been rubbing body butter into my breasts to avoid stretchmarks and at 34 weeks pregnant, I found the lump. It was as awful as you'd imagine...disbelief, fear, heartbreak. When our daughter was born 4 weeks early, I was utterly terrified of loving her, because I was convinced I was going to have to leave her. But I remember that tug of love in my stomach when she was born and I remember knowing she was going to get me through anything - and I was going to get myself through anything I had to in order to stay for her.

When she was 6 days old, I had a mastectomy and a few weeks later came the brutal chemo where my nails peeled off and my hair fell out and nausea consumed my entire life. I spent my maternity leave back in the Oncology department where I also worked! Thankfully after a year of falling even more deeply in love our little Ivy, we got the words we had been desperate for; remission!!!! There is no greater feeling than hearing those words after looking death in the eye. I created a living list - things I wanted to do in this one and wonderful life. We went on holidays and we applied to adopt a son. We were approved in November 2017. In January while we were waiting to be matched with a child, I found another lump.

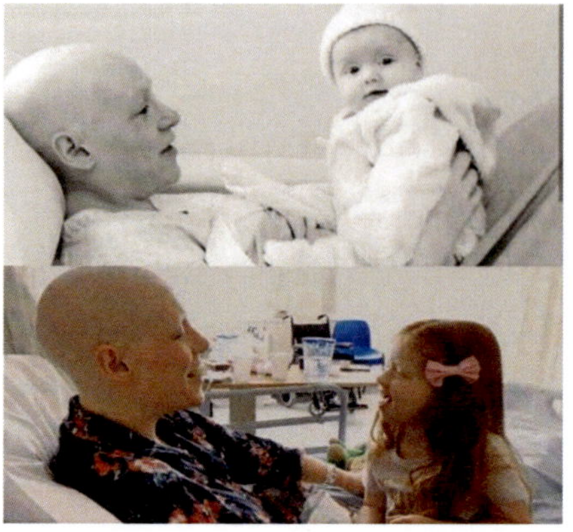

I can't ever forget the feeling of hot oil being poured through my blood, the lurching of my stomach, the instant tears in my eyes. The glance at Ivy who's 3 now and I look at my husband and he says "what's wrong?"

My 2nd diagnosis: it wasn't some neat Hollywood moment where the Dr sits you down and tells you what's going to happen. It was "I don't think you've understood our conversation properly Roisin, we're no longer looking at a cure for you." It was snot and clenched fistfuls of Michael's jumper. It was anger that my concerns had been ignored for months. It was shattering heartbreak and a feeling of such isolation knowing in that moment not one human being on earth could tell me it was going to be okay. I looked at Michael and I wanted to beg him to help me, but I knew that he couldn't. He knew it, too.

I left the room that day without a single ounce of hope. I was dying and they wanted to 'manage my expectations.' I just remember the absolute despair. The agony of looking at my 3-year-old daughter. My best friend in the whole world - and I was hers, too! I kept saying over and over and over. I can't leave her, I can't, I can't, I can't. I could not accept it.

From that pit of darkness, eventually, came a crack of light and from that light came determination. Knowing that I would do anything it took to LIVE for my girl. It wasn't just my life at risk, it was hers too. What would her life look like without me? Who'll do her hair for school when she's big enough? The questions I had to ask myself shattered my heart into pieces, a pain I can't even begin to describe...but meeting women in the secondary cancer community was such a gift. For a long time, I had felt like I was drowning alone but now there was someone in the water with me and they were holding my hand helping me stay afloat. F2BH brought into my life some spectacular women. These women, living the same sentence as me were the most alive women I had ever met. They had plans, defiance and dreams. They wanted to squeeze every last drop out of life and I wanted in!

Among those women was Kate Orr, our Queen Kate. She is the kind of woman who deserves a film made about her; Kate has this rare mix of fire and compassion. She will fight for you as fiercely as she fights for herself, and she has carried this charity on her back with a determination that still leaves me wondering how she does it. Where others might have folded under the weight of grief and exhaustion, Kate channelled it into purpose. She saw the gaps, the silence around secondary breast cancer and decided she wouldn't stand for it. She created something that the rest of us could lean on. Something that gave us a voice. Something that said: we are still here, and we matter.

When you see Kate in action, you know you're witnessing someone extraordinary. She's relentless, she's clever, and she has a way of pulling people together that makes you believe change really is possible. She didn't just build Fighting to be Heard; she built a family. For me, being part of that family is such a gift. I may not be the one leading the charge, but standing alongside Kate and my girls, adding my voice to theirs, has given me strength I never knew I had. Kate reminds me every day that even when cancer tries to silence us, we can still roar.

My Life Now

Seven years on from being handed a three-year prognosis, I'm still here. When I was first told there was no cure, I thought my world had ended. But the truth is, a new world began. A world where every single day matters. A world where I don't wait around for permission or for "the right time." I made a Living List back then - all the things I wanted to see, do, feel and become while I had the chance. And instead of it gathering dust in a drawer, I started ticking things off. Sometimes the big things, sometimes the tiny ones that mean the most.

We bought a camper van - Cherry Bomb Diggity - and she's taken us on adventures that make my heart full to the brim with gratitude. We've slept under the stars, woken up by the sea, and watched sunsets I thought I might never see. I started a podcast, because I realised my voice matters even if it wobbles, even if I go off on tangents. It matters because it's real. I built a small business that's grown into more than I ever dreamed, sending little pieces of hope and cheek out into the world.

And through it all, I've had my family. Michael by my side, Ivy now a brilliant little human who once saved my life just by being born, and Leo, who completed us in ways I didn't even know we needed. My friends old and new, the ones I found through cancer, the ones the Universe nudged into my path have become family too.

So, here I am. Not cured. Not out of the woods. But living a life in HD, and soaking up every last drop of it. And if you take anything from my story, let it be this: life doesn't stop because of a diagnosis. It changes, yes. It sharpens. But it can still expand in ways you never imagined.

CHAPTER 20

CATHY SNAPE

Written by Sean Snape, Cathys Husband

How do you encapsulate a person and their life, to do justice to their story, their legacy and to capture the essence of your loved one...retrospectively? That was the dilemma I had before me when asked to write a chapter about Cathy and her time with this amazing bunch of people! So the challenge is how to write something that can help to inform and educate the readers about the reality of living and ultimately dying from secondary breast cancer?

As the book will already have explained the origins of the exceptional day in September 2021 when 20 incredible and courageous women all met up for the first time on that fateful day, I will share some of my memories and observations on Cathy's behalf.

The condensed synopsis version of Cathy's cancer discovery and treatment will be familiar to so many people, a suspicion lump in her armpit, a sense of unease and feeling unwell and a sixth sense that 'something wasn't right' led her to seek medical advice. In early January 2021 she went to our GP surgery, who were amazing and rushed things through as best they could. As you've probably guessed from the date, we were in the middle of the pandemic!

She was seen very quickly, blood tests and biopsy were done, scans rushed through and then the dreaded call to come and speak to the GP. Stage 4 secondary breast cancer with numerous lesions on her liver. Sitting in that office was one of the hardest moments of my life and to say its a bit of a blur would be an understatement...I can't testify to what Cathy felt at hearing the news and I hope I'm not coming across as dismissive in my recounting of that day, there will others in this book who will have given their reaction to hearing such devastating news...the million and one questions that spring to mind, or the sheer numbness and inability to process what you are being told. There will be a huge span of emotions and feelings to contend with and unless you have been on the receiving end of such devastating news, I don't think you or I can begin to grasp the pivotal life changing enormity of that moment. She took the news as best she could and in her typical Cathy style went on the offensive, ignored the advice not to Google the diagnosis and threw herself into understanding what was going on and to be informed for when she saw the oncologist.

Nothing can change the fact though that after a difficult conversation like that, the experience is generally the same for everyone...feeling like the rug has been pulled out from underneath you, experiencing information overload, bombarded with terminology and jargon that you mostly have no idea what they are saying, scary sounding treatments and procedures...oh an here's some leaflets and links to help answer any questions, ring if you need anything and we'll see you soon. Generally there is a designated point of contact, the breast care nurse to liaise and answer your questions, but being the NHS, these wonderful people are stretched thin, covering many other patients and often not able to pick up when you ring, either out of office, or with another patient. So this rapport you try to build with this person, I say rapport, it's more like clinging onto a friendly face whilst barely treading water, slowly drowning in the enormity of what is going on, is unavailable, so you make do with whoever can answer your frantic questions, if something feels wrong or your anxiety levels are off the scale. I will refer back to this support need later in the chapter.

From the start Cathy responded fantastically to the medication, shrinkage to almost zero the size of the lesions on her liver, manageable side effects and she was able to keep her hair, though it thinned out alarmingly in a very short space of time. She was what is affectionately termed in the group as a 'Stable Mabel' and so we arrive at the catalyst that is her introduction to our special group of ladies, enter stage right.

I must confess at this stage that I am not 100% sure how Cathy's path crossed with our gang of girls, whether it was a recommendation by Macmillan to join Make Seconds Count forum, or some deep diving that Cathy did, looking for local cancer patients to support and link with, in an effort to make sense of what she was going through and to fill her free time and to help find distractions from being left with her own thoughts and fears. However she found them and I will forever be grateful that she did!

From my perspective, when your loved one gets struck down by this evil, cruel and indiscriminate disease, you find yourself on the outside looking in. Your automatic reflex is to make it all better, or to take it away from your loved one...somehow make everything alright...and we can't! All you can do is sit on the sidelines whilst you watch your loved one rant and rage through that maelstrom of emotions, never knowing which one will strike next, whether it's something as triggering as intrusive thoughts that you'll never see your daughter walk down the aisle, or help her with her first child. Whether it's the unfairness of this disease choosing her, when so many plans were in motion to enjoy her later years, all snatched away with the reality of a secondary cancer diagnosis. Mapping out what the next six months would look like, 12 months, 2 years, please God let me have 3 so I can see our daughter graduate Uni, to be there to share her cap and gown moment. Seeing her grandkids grow up. See the middle child settle down and find someone to love. The list is endless and speaks to everyone in this horrible situation.

As someone who could only watch from the sidelines as these raw and often overwhelming feelings raged, to say you feel useless and helpless is putting it mildly. It's so easy to say the wrong thing at the wrong time, trying to reassure and pass comment on things that you can't ever comprehend, trying to rationalise or show support, but saying it the wrong way, or more often than not, saying something kind or loving, that resonates with them that triggers grief and emotion that they'd managed to hold in up until you spoke, highlighting how deeply they feel or are hurting. You end up being stuck in limbo, afraid to say anything as whatever is said will likely not help the situation...but guess what... you still do!

One of the hardest things Cathy had to contend with and kept this to herself until much later on in her trials and tribulations, was the isolation of not feeling like she could talk to anyone about what she was feeling, facing and going through...in stepped our little gang of heroines! to say that this small group of women helped to keep her sane and able to put one foot in front of the other and face whatever fell in her path is an understatement. She described it to me as 'finding her tribe' when she first contacted this small support group, she was able to speak to and voice her fears and terrors with others who just 'Got it' No filters, No topics off limit, No judgement and No repercussions for whatever was said...she found a band of sisters who she could say all that she couldn't say to her nearest and dearest.

Why couldn't she tell these things, share these worries and fears with her nearest and dearest you might be wondering, a sentiment I thought of often, in the beginning! She would be sat in bed, messaging away, sometimes furiously tapping away on her tablet or laptop, sometimes in the wee small hours on her phone, deep in a conversation thread, often seen with a tear or two rolling down her cheeks, but more often than not with a shy smile or a look of gratitude as she's receiving messages from these women she had never met or at that point, even spoken to. She shared with me that these women helped her to navigate her way through the darkness that she felt was trying to engulf her, that these strangers welcomed her with open arms into a gang that no one wants to be a part of, that no amount of incentive would ever entice you to join, but once you were in, you felt welcomed, listened to and loved, that you could tell these strangers exactly how you were feeling, how scared you were, how alone and isolated you felt, even while surrounded by friends and family and they all understood and just 'Got It'. From asking the difficult questions around treatment rounds, side effects, what had worked for some and not for others, to find someone who was six months into the treatment that she was just starting, being able to ask if this reaction was normal, if this was how it felt, to find others who could reassure her that it was okay, or signpost her to alternative remedies that would help bring her some comfort or relief from some of the more painful reactions and side effects, helped Cathy to normalise the whole process. It gave her a safety net that no one else could, it normalised what she was going through and gave her some semblance of balance and control in a world that must at times have felt like a helter skelter that she was plummeting down at a hundred miles an hour. This lifeline was the support that

she was able to cling too and gain comfort and reassurance by being with those in the same boat...i mentioned earlier about the designated point of contact provided by the oncology team, this group of women have taken on that role and are supporting their own, to try and stop or help pause those overwhelming sinking feelings, to be the aid to cancel out those feelings of slowly drowning and barely treading water.

I describe this amazing band of women as the family you never knew you needed and definitely never wanted. There is a shared camaraderie , a shared misery, dread and laughter in the face of adversity...someone to turn too in the middle of the night and offload, or unburden to, able to say the things you can't say to your loved ones...a sisterhood of support, people who understands the dreads and sleepless nights wrestling with the night time terrors that sneak up on you, when you are feeling all alone with your thoughts, thoughts that are too overwhelming to articulate and share with those closest to you.

As the story unfolds in the book, you will have heard how the group decided to meet up and do something, to raise awareness and to fight to have their silenced voices heard, to stop being marginalised as patients, be acknowledged and not be cast aside. The goal was to shine a light on the plight of secondary breast cancer, to highlight that there are no long term winners in this, no survivors in this group, no bells to be rung when remission is reached, no end to the treatment and moving on with lives, just the certainty that a holding action is the best that can be hoped for and a need to rush through all and any drug and treatment trials to help in any way, to stave off the relentless push of the cancer cells trying to kill you! One day a blessed cure will be found, but until that day, don't write off those living with the diagnosis!

Meeting that wonderful band of women, spending time with them really helped me to join the dots and to understand why this group was so important, why this small group of people had joined together to support and lift each other up, to be there for each other, initially as strangers sharing a common cause, living with secondary breast cancer and all that simple three word diagnosis would come to mean to them. As I mentioned earlier, there is no clique or gang, or tribe that anyone wants to join, no incentive would ever entice you to be a part of this...and yet once you join, there's no looking back! There is no finer group of friends to guide you, inform and hold you up, when you feel dragged down to your lowest point.

But, as always, the villain of the piece had never left, was still lurking with intent and was quietly bidding its time, waiting for its opportunity to strike back...it was postponed, or set back, but it had no intention of being beaten. We will never know how the cancer spread, whether it was the fact that Cathy was hospitalised overnight with a bad dose of Covid, that led to her immune system being weakened or whether she was just unlucky and the cancer had found a way to circumvent the successful treatments and spread exponentially. All we do know is that Cathy felt out of sorts around Christmas 2021, something wasn't right. She'd gone through the rollercoaster of yet another round of 'Scanxiety' and had a clean bill of health early December, her bloods consistently came back as clear, scan showed no causes for concern. The oncology department reduced her treatment program to reflect how well she had responded to the treatment and had reduced the frequency of her blood screening, so confident they were in her successful response to the chemotherapy.

What happened then in the weeks and months to follow was a rollercoaster ride, that never seemed to end, a revolving door of admittance to A&E initially, then after that we would bypass the front door and be rushed in through the back, either to general admittance, or to the Oncology ward, bed availability permitting. I lost track of how many hospital trips we made, how many times I would be unable to be with her in her hours of need, Bloody Covid messed everything up. One of the low points was standing outside in the pouring rain, talking through an inch gap from the open window, wearing a mask and listening to the registrar giving her yet another bout of bad news. I wasn't alone, on my left was another relative talking to his partner through her ground floor suite window...you couldn't make this stuff up, even fiction writers wouldn't have come up with this as a scene in a film. Yet there we were, making the best of it in unprecedented times.

One memorable admittance that stands out and is important to share is an early A&E admittance with serious breathing difficulties. Fluid on the lungs was the cause and a suction procedure was being arranged, when a consultant walked into the bay. He looked at her chart and with a perplexed expression on his face turned to Cathy and asked, in my opinion a rather callous and offhand way, if she wanted the fluid draining...if she was comfortable and with a DNR in place, was it what she needed? Wouldn't she much rather be discharged and go home?

Two things instantly leapt to my mind...why is he suggesting that the treatment is a choice and up for debate whether she wants or needs it and secondly DNR!!! It's fluid on the lung!! In its early stages, it's generally not considered life-threatening or fatal by any stretch of the imagination. She had been admitted with difficulty breathing, suspected fluid on the lungs and a probable infection here with no mention of suspected pneumonia or pleurisy, she was reasonably fit and active, as healthy as can be expected after undergoing a successful round of chemotherapy treatment and, being in her mid fifties, hardly ready to be written off and considered to be in her twilight years!!! A DNR...WTF!!!

To say conflicting emotions wrestled to the surface and no doubt onto our shocked faces would be an understatement. He swiftly read the room and started backtracking around the fact that a DNR was a standard response to a secondary breast cancer diagnosis, that it was a terminal diagnosis and therefore a DNR would routinely be placed on a patient's file. Shocked and horrified are two words that barely do justice to hearing such offhand and thoughtless comments. This experience though difficult and challenging in so many ways, also brought it home to me the views around secondary breast cancer and hearing the experiences of so many others, whether it's the attitude that isn't most cancers curable by now, or the fact that you don't look like your ill, let alone dying, or the upbeat stories around the successful treatment and remission results for so many lucky 'survivors' and the assumption that most people who have finished the treatment cycle and are Stable Mabels are somehow in the clear. The harsh reality for secondary breast cancer sufferers is that there are no 'Survivor' accolades, no oncology bells to ring when treatment is finished, no end to this evil condition, just as mentioned before, a holding action to keep the cancer in check. Please do not think I am in any way disrespecting or downplaying anyone's cancer and treatment ordeals, nothing could be further from the truth, but these misconceptions around SBC are the reason why there is the need to be heard and a recognition that anyone with a SBC is not at this moment in time on the receiving end of the 'happily ever after' that so many fortunate others are.

What followed was the revolving door of hospital admissions, often for days at a time, intravenous antibiotics trying to tackle the fluid buildup worsening on her lungs, more scans, more draining of fluid, being hooked up to a ventilator and then on oxygen. She was eventually discharged home under the palliative care team and set up to have an oxygen machine at home.

This is where ignorance and lack of understanding of what was happening plays a part in what happened next. The rationale behind being sent home was, as we understood it, that once the lung infection was under control, Cathy could start some form of cancer treatment to tackle the rampaging, unchecked cancer that had free roaming access. At this stage it was rooted firmly in her lungs, lymphatic system and suspected in her bones and spine, to finally end up in her brain. However, it was explained to us that once the infection was under control, radiotherapy treatment would be started to try and shrink the various clusters of cells, but that Cathy had to be strong enough to take on the rigours of the treatments..

The reality was that she would not be strong enough to start any treatment, that it was too far advanced and past the point where any treatment would be effective. Sadly, we were not aware of this and in our desperate need to cling onto any hope of recovery or staving off the inevitable, we were blissfully unaware of the reality of her situation. Looking back our naivety and ignorance was almost childlike, whether it was not asking the difficult questions, or not understanding the wider picture, or that it wasn't explained to us properly, is something I have thought long and hard about, since those dark times. One of the rationales behind this book is to try and inform and educate those following along behind the girls we have lost, to learn from the ordeals they faced and try and steer others away from these pitfalls that we fell down. There were so many clues happening at the time that should have been picked up on, but we didn't. Having Cathy discharged to the palliative care team, was the first one, having a syringe driver fitted to manage her medications, primarily Oramorph and other dangerous medication is another. District nurses were coming in every day to change the medications, monitor her breathing and oxygen levels as well as check in on her general health. When the offer of hospice respite was suggested, with the view to manage her meds effectively, have a proper trained team to care for her, as we understood it as a short term intervention, to get her match fit to start radiotherapy, we jumped at the chance.

Things were looking up, she was looking forward to getting the right care and attention, to get her strong enough and ready to start the next stage of her cancer journey. As everyone knows, who are dealing with this horrendous situation, there are always options available...Cathy had only endured her first line of treatment, there would be others available to explore to hopefully hold back the cancer spread. We had always understood that there were new and exciting treatments coming through all the time, that there were several stages of treatment and as one stopped being effective, another would be used to try and hold back the cancer onslaught.

We were in for a massive wake up call and a life changing conversation, that I can safely say turned our world upside down. We had safely got Cathy set up in the lovely hospice suite, all hooked up to the state of the art monitoring equipment and had just had her induction for want of a better word and just generally chatting with the hospice manager and nurse. Cathy, ever practical, had moved the conversation onto the topic of her treatment to help her stabilise and regain her strength and resilience to start looking towards starting a radiotherapy treatment and asked if she would be staying here and transported back and forth to the oncology ward, just really ironing out the logistics. We had been told that the radiotherapy would have to be accessed from a different hospital to the one she was under, some 20 miles further away and wanted to get all her ducks lined up. We were told that the hospice consultant would be round to see her shortly and she and I could have a chat with him.

We met the consultant and, being on a roll, started asking all those questions that had been deferred until his arrival. He very gently and softly broke the news to us that there would be no radiotherpy treatment. He carefully and tactfully explained to us the reason Cathy had been transferred to the hospice, was because her battle with cancer had sadly come to an end, that she was at ST Davids to make her as comfortable as possible and to give her the dignity and care she would need at this late stage of her life. They were there to see to her palliative end of life care, to manage her pain relief and to offer her a dignified and calm environment, to support her and the family through this difficult time and that in his experience we would have a week to ten days at best before Cathy would pass away.

I'll pause there for a moment to let that sink in...this was obviously a million miles away from the chat we were expecting. Time seemed to stand still as this revelation registered and everything changed in a heartbeat. Cathy and I were left alone to process what had been said and to just try and comfort each other, as best we could. You would think a moment like that would trigger a million questions, that so many conflicting emotions would be wrestling and overwhelming you in equal measure, but to say there was an eerie calm, would be the best way to describe those few minutes. We sat together in silence, each swept up in our own thoughts and feelings, just holding hands and letting everything sink in.

My first thought, after seeing to Cathy's immediate needs was how do I tell the kids. How do you break the news to the family and what on earth are we supposed to do! I don't really remember much after that, there were lots of follow on conversations that day, around making Cathy comfortable, visiting options because of Covid, practical suggestions around registering a death etc, some pamphlets were given and probably lots of other things discussed. I don't know what Cathy was feeling when she was told the news, we never really had a chance to talk about it together and nothing would alter the fact of being told that she had at best a week to settle her affairs and say her goodbyes.

Through those first four days Cathy's health deteriorated, fluid on the lung was causing complications and she started presenting signs of confusion and agitation. She was tired, exhausted and tired of fighting and with the timeline given, became obsessed with knowing how long she had left, how much more she had to endure, just wanting it to be over and to be allowed to let her go. Every time the medical staff checked in on her, the first thing she would ask would be how long till she would die. I tried my hardest to spare any of the family hearing her pleas, no one should hear a loved one begging to be given something to ease them towards death, or to have them beg you to put them out of their misery. Euthanasia is an emotive subject, widely controversial and divisive for so many reasons, but from a personal point of view, for the sake of someone's dignity and right to control their own lives, I believe we should have a way to be more humane in our care for the terminally ill.

Further tests were conducted and it was determined that the brain was the latest host that the cancer had spread to and that she was starting to present signs of paraneoplastic encephalitis (I've had to Google her symptoms and come up with the most likely culprit as I can't recall what we were told) she started presenting dementia like behaviour, agitation, distress, fight or flight impulses that led to her trying to unhook herself on several occasions and to try and escape from her bed. In her weakened state she would have seriously harmed herself and potentially others who would be tasked to keep her safe, so the decision was made to sedate her. That should have been the end of the story, a quick decline in a sedated state and to just slip away quietly. But fate chose to take another turn.

A different consultant was called to see how best to help make Cathy comfortable and to aid in her presented dementia symptoms and he took a different approach. He actioned the continuation of the fluid removal from her lungs and a change in medication, which had a miraculous effect within 24 hours. We had Cathy return to us. Weakened and frail but more aware and with her faculties back and the confusion and agitation vanished.

With this change of circumstances they had to revise Cathy's original timelines and they offered a tentative extension.

With this news and feeling more like her old self, she had a request, a final wish if you will, that we try and take her back home to Carno to be near her family and her childhood stomping ground. Phone calls and emails were sent to Powys local health authority and a transfer was arranged. That sentence can't begin to do justice to what that meant to Cathy and her family, how grateful we were for so much compassion and kindness being shown.

Cathy was known to the team at the local cottage hospital in

Llanidloes that kindly offered their hospice suite for Cathy to be moved too, the head nurse and two of the senior staff were lifelong friends who had all grown up together, whose children had gone to school where Cathy had worked and looked after them in the local nursery that she worked in...they wanted her to come home to be among her own and to be looked after by them. Words cannot begin to express the gratitude and love I feel towards those angels in nurses uniforms! From the moment we were told it could happen and who was involved in offering to care for her, a lightness came over Cathy and an inner peace seemed to descend.

I'm acutely aware that stories have a way of getting away from the author, once they start tapping away at the keyboard, so I will try and simplify as much as I can the last few days after the successful transfer to the cottage hospital. From the moment in the hospice when we had received the devastating news, there had been a fatalistic attitude that had seemed to deflate and quash the Cathy we knew and loved, but with this move and the prospect of going home, she was revitalised and in true Cathy style, it gave her the impetus and the resolve to go out on her terms. Phone calls were made to the local vicar of her home village, visits were arranged to discuss the funeral service, undertaker known to the family came and arrangements were finalised, all under Cathy's watchful, if tired and weary eyes. The order of service was arranged and delegated to Chloe to prepare, music for the service was chosen, a burial plot arranged and flowers discussed. A resolve to have some say in how her final hurrah would play out empowered her and gave her a feeling of control, in a world where that had been taken away from her. Precious time was spent with family and friends, the children were offered a holiday cottage by one of Cathy's friends for the duration of the time we needed it, so they could all be there on hand for her final few days. She was able to speak candidly to her family and lay to rest old wrongs that she felt had been left unresolved...in short she was able to get most of her affairs in order.

Sadly, there was one aspect of this control that was slipping away, faster than she wished and that was her voice, or more specifically, her ability to be able to express herself and say what she needed to say. The side effects from the ever strengthening doses of Olymorph and the other meds, along with whatever carnage the cancer was causing in her brain, were rapidly taking away her cognitive abilities. She had a wish to write a keepsake note to all the family, something personal and of meaning from her for them to remember her by and to read from time to time. The first note she started writing, she lost the ability to hold the pen, let alone use it to write anything and it caused a great amount of pain and anguish for her, railing against the fact that she had left it too late to say what needed to be said and to write what she needed to write. It was tasked to me and Chloe to try and help her to fulfil her wish. I found it a very difficult task, uncomfortable in being the pen that wrote down her heartfelt and often painful messages to her loved ones, frustrated that it had been left too late to have been done in her distinctive handwriting, that would have meant so much more as a keepsake and to make matters worse, Cathy started losing her ability to speak. Known as one of the side effects of Oramorph this caused no end of heartache for Cathy and led to frustration and upset as she tried to articulate what she needed to say, but was steadily losing the ability to do so. Chloe did a fantastic job trying to help Cathy to articulate the word she might be looking for, but as we went on Cathy was struggling to remember the words and even say them out loud, losing strength in her vocal cords and the whole process took many hours to finish. Just to clarify, we are not talking about writing war and peace for each family member, these were small notelets of meaningful and heartfelt messages of gratitude, love and appreciation for the life she had led with these loved ones, whether it was her parents, her siblings or the hardest ones to write...to her children. Chloe helped out with some, but there was a time when she had to be absent from the exercise as it was too painful and distressing for Cathy to have her daughter see her in that way. We muddled through and got them written, with the express instruction that I give them out at the funeral. It took everything out of her, the tank was empty at this point, all her reserves were used up in seeing to the plans and messages for her final time with us. She left my note till last and I'm saddened to say, we never managed to write one. She valiantly tried to hold the pen and write it herself, but it was beyond her ability at that stage. She had pretty much lost her ability to speak, drifting in and out of consciousness and we were losing more and more lucid moments with her.

A bitter sweet moment followed, our granddaughter's birthday was due in a couple of days and in one of Cathy's lucid moments, she insisted that the family go off for the day to celebrate... understandable no one was in the mood for a party, but she insisted that they carry on as normal and go off to ten pin bowling and have a meal out, go have some fun and enjoy themselves. Now, I am no expert on these things, but I have spoken to a handful of people who work in end of life care and the consensus has been that there is with some people an awareness of when their time is up and when they are ready to go, they will have their affairs in order and pass away peacefully. As I have mentioned previously, Cathy was done in, she had fought enough and just wanted it to be over with, the questions around when she would be dying persisted right up until her ability to ask stopped, so there was no doubt about her mindset.

She passed away, peacefully and swiftly, within a couple of hours of them leaving, I would like to think that it was on her terms and to her timeframe.

Cathy loved parties, children's parties especially and to mark our granddaughters birthday, a party was organised for that evening, all the nieces and nephews, cousins would be there, little ones running around, just as Cathy would have loved. So a party was held, a celebration of a little girl's 4th birthday. It was a chance for everyone to be together and to quietly grieve and to mark her passing by raising a glass and shedding a quiet tear. The children ran around excited, oblivious to the situation, innocent in their joy of being together, running around and eating too much cake and whatnot...and rightly so...it's what Cathy would have hoped for and deserved as her final happy get together.

As this chapter has come to its natural end with Cathy's passing I'm left with the task of summing up and adding my thoughts and to the message I'm wanting to convey for the book and the F2BH cause. I have touched on the many ways Cathy felt connected with this extraordinary sisterhood, how they help and support each other and my abiding closing thoughts are around these women.

Cathy has left her own legacy in the life she led, the lives and people she touched and connected with, but her story was tragically cut short, silenced before its time. She and sadly so many others can no longer shout, or fight tooth and nail to be heard.

So we have to do it in their memory, in their stead, step up and be their voices, fight for their words to be heard. There is a song by Sam Ryder that strikes a cord with me, called 'Tiny Riot' and it always sends shivers down my spine when I hear it.

One of the lines goes:

In the darkness there's a light
You can find it if you try
If you open up your eyes
If your drifting out to sea
You can just hold on to me
We'll make it to the other side

And then the chorus kicks in, which I'll come to in a moment.

I think of Cathy when I hear this verse, imagining her reaching out in the dark of night, when she felt at her most scared and alone and feeling helpless and afraid and I like to imagine these lyrics encapsulate how she felt when she found her tribe, her special sisterhood, her extraordinary family and how they helped her, stopped her drifting away alone and just held her close as they navigated the seas together.

In the words of the chorus:

Mothers, Sisters, Fathers, Brother, step into the light and start a Tiny Riot

Stop being so goddamn quiet, got a spark in your heart so strike it.

Wash away your pain, turn the pouring rain to a tidal wave and ride it.

Got something inside don't hide it, like dynamite ignite it
wash away your pain, turn the pouring rain to the wave of a tiny riot

Cathy never managed to start a hurricane, ride a tidal wave, or start her Tiny Riot.

But the responsibility that has been passed onto us, by those who have sadly been silenced must live on and We must be the ones to Fight to Be Heard in their name and memory.

In Loving Memory

08.06.2022

CHAPTER 21

LESLEY GRAINEY

From Barnsley to Breast Cancer

Hi my name is Lesley and I am originally from Barnsley. I was diagnosed with Secondary Breast Cancer in August 2018. I was 47.

I have 2 children; Ailsa who is now 13, and Mackenzie who is 15. I am very grateful to have two teenage kids, as when I was diagnosed, they were 7 and 9.

I am married to Jack, we live in Shoreham by Sea, and we have a campervan called Jaffa.

At the moment, I work at the same secondary school that my kids go to as the Head of Drama.

I have been living with cancer for 6 years now and I am on my first line of treatment.

First of all, how weird is this? How can something as shocking as getting secondary breast cancer have me now trying to write about my story in a book within a charity I am a founder of?

Since being diagnosed with secondary breast cancer on August the 16th 2018, my life has been complicated, stressful, emotional, and at times like these very bizarre. I am approaching my 6 year anniversary since my secondary diagnosis and it's a big deal.

I am not sure if on that day when I was told that my cancer was now incurable, and life limiting, I actually saw anything beyond death. Certainly, I had no understanding of living with cancer, I saw no future; stage 4 cancer to me at the time was the end of the end. So, to be writing this is very bizarre, overwhelming and another reminder that you just don't know what's around the corner.

The year I was diagnosed with cancer, 2018, I was the fittest I had ever been, and was due to run the Brighton marathon 10 years after losing my Dad to bowel cancer. He had retired at 65, was diagnosed at 66, and died at 67. I wanted to mark not having him around for 10 years and support Marie Curie, whose nurses had been like angels on earth during the last few days of his life.

It's January 2018, I'd had bumps around my breast and had very big boobs; I mean they were fantastic! But they were huge, and my usual bra size was 30FF. I had already had two scares in my life when I found lumps and they came to nothing; so I had some experience. In hindsight, I was going through early menopause and was struggling with so much unexplained stuff. So, for me I think cancer and the menopause collided like "The Big Bang" around this time, and I never had a chance to really know what was going on.

So, I had bumps around my breast but as far as I could feel nothing in the breast. Two doctors suggested antibiotics and maybe that's what I wanted to hear. Big boobs, tight sports bra; it made sense.

I know when I did find a lump in my breast; it was in April, on my husband's birthday. I remember we were in the motorhome at the time, camping for his birthday. It was a drizzly day, we were near Margate, and I found the lump in my breast. Even though we were on holiday, I remember having to do a really long marathon training run that morning. 18 miles or something. I just thought it can't be anything serious, you can't be ill if you are doing a marathon. How silly, how naive – cancer doesn't give a shit!!

I remember thinking if it's still there after the marathon, I'll go and get it checked out. I remember laying down on the massage table after the marathon and having my legs done; I was on my tummy and I could feel the lump in my breast and I kind of got scared then. I got it checked out with the doctors, even taking both kids to the appointment! Straight away, they placed me on the waiting list to go to the breast clinic.

Fast forward, I go to the breast clinic they take biopsies, and on 24th May 2018 it was confirmed I had cancer. ER positive, HER2 negative, grade 2, invasive ductal. Initially we thought it was primary, and we had so many bloody leaflets I can't tell you; I had a whole A5 ring file on cancer. At the time I actually thought this will be alright. I could do a shit year. The boobs had served me well. I had a lovely husband, and they had fed my two amazing children; If my boobs had to go because they were killing me, then fine.

In July, and in the words of the "Spice Girls" it was the day "When two became One"; losing a boob is weird. They actually use a marker pen on your chest to point out the boob that needed to go. When I woke up from the operation, I didn't even have to look at my chest I knew one had gone the difference in weight was incredible. At this point there was no chat about reconstruction or anything; let's just get the cancer. Some of my lymph nodes had to go too.

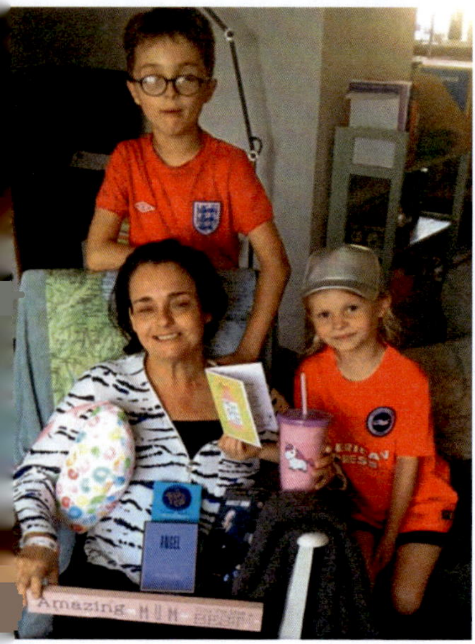

It's a funny time of having pillows to go under your arms, mobility exercises, and those very tight socks. This was the first part of "I am ill". I was so glad that the cancer had been taken away, but having an udder with one boob was really tricky. Things will never be the same again. (another Spice Girls quote). This began "The new normal".

More scans after the mastectomy to see what chemo I was going to have. It was then that we found out my cancer that had started in my breast had crept into the lymph nodes (these are the 'Bouncers' or door men in your body), before going past them into another part of the body. It was just to one place (limited spread categorised as oligometastatic) but it now meant the cancer was classified as Stage 4.

It was 16th August 2018. The oncologist told us, who to say wasn't blessed with a great bedside manner would be an understatement, but I didn't actually listen to the whole of the chat and had to leave the room. In fact it was my husband who tried to take in the information and ask the BIG question. So how long? It was explained to him that basically stage 4 cancer was like progressing up a ladder of treatments. Once one finished you moved to the next until there was no more.

If you google it, it said three to five years life expectancy. We only saw that oncologist once, we asked to change to someone else after that. The telling of such a diagnosis is something that I really feel we need to be better at.

The only cancer I had seen face-to-face was with my dad; an image I find difficult to remove from my memory, it was full of horror and anguish. The cancer had eaten away at him, leaving a shell of a man I loved and admired, who I continued to miss every day. That was my thought in this moment, and that was my vision. That was going to happen to me. I thought my Dad was young at 67, and how difficult the impact of cancer had been on me; and here I was at 47, looking down the barrel of a stage 4 cancer diagnosis. But it's not just me looking at my own mortality, it's everyone around you. My amazing husband had to carry this too, and still does day in, day out.

One of the first things I did with my mum after the news was to wrap gifts for the children, something of mine with a birthday card, until they were 21. I guessed I would live for 4 years so Mack's first gift from me was for his 13th birthday, and Ailsa for her 11th until her 21st. These were tough times.

There had been no need to get my hair cut into a bob style, getting ready for losing my hair, as I wasn't going to. Those images of cancer patients wasn't going to be me. The pink and fluffy, the survivor story, the 'you've got this', the ringing the bell; the life after. All of that wasn't going to be my story.

My medication was tablet based, and since August 2018, I have been on my first line of treatment. At the time, a relatively new drug called Palbociclib was available; you take one every day - 3 weeks on, one week off.

Everyday, I also take Letrozole, which gets rid of Oestrogen, which basically means you are in a constant state of menopause, with no chance of HRT.

Denosumab is a bone strengthener, which I get every 2 months as an injection.

The year that followed was a blur; I was in an obvious panic to have it all, everything and anything to help. Lots of jokes, about the singer "Prince" having a rib removed, so surely if he could do it, so could I, and then we would have got rid of the cancer. It doesn't really work like that.

I said yes to Radiotherapy around where the cancer had been. I didn't realise this would then stop any possibility of implants, but it was the least of my worries. As well as scars, a wobbly arm, no feeling at the back of my arm as they cut tendons to get rid of lymph nodes, I now had a collection of small black marks; little tattoos that they used to line up the radiotherapy machines.

There was research, and counselling, and changes in diet; no alcohol, juicing, lots and lots of celery, supplements, thoughts of going to Mexico for some retreat, second opinions, just a lot. On top of that was the mental journey; every morning and every night, going to bed thinking I have cancer, I am going to die, I am not going to see my kids grow up. Round and round and round. That was just the never-ending loop of 'Why me?', it's my fault. There wasn't a part of my being that wasn't affected by this diagnosis and like a pebble being dropped in still water, the ripple effects of cancer affected everyone around me.

There seemed to be a change, when I thought it was primary to when it became secondary; a bit of a dirty secret surrounding the "Ones we can't cure". We found help and support away from the NHS with Macmillan and the Horizon centre in Brighton. What a godsend they were; I went to the centre and fell apart in the foyer, literally like a big puddle of a mess of a human being. Tears overflowing. They scooped me and Jack up, and gave us access to so much support, for which we will be forever grateful.

Having an invisible disease is a weird one, I look fine, but carry, well, drag this massive thing with me all the time. The energy and thought it takes to be and act fine, is a bloody full-time job; being ok is a big deal. They say it's 'OK to not be OK', but hey, if I didn't work hard on the OK thing then I would just stop and that's not an option. We all have our shit and once you walk into the room that is cancer, it is full; full of people, full of affected people, full of people who have it worse than me. We all have our shit, some of it is called cancer, some of it is called other stuff, but in every family, every friendship group everyone has their thing.

Mine is secondary breast cancer, what's yours?

The first year was a bit of a blur, and now I am on my daily intake of drugs and supplements, and 3 month scans; and 'Scanxiety' is a thing. A massive thing that builds up before the scan and then there is the waiting. Other people know how well you are but you don't. Going into the room with the oncologist starting a bit of chit-chat, usually with the opening line 'How are you?' and me with 'I don't know! You tell me! Stop talking!' screaming in my head; all I want to know is 'AM I STABLE?'.

I am fortunate that so far I have been stable; however, I have had my fair share of scares. They saw something in my bowel, another time in my lymph nodes; all these need investigating. As I write this, they have seen something in my lungs. We wait and see; someone already knows what that is about, but I don't yet.

So, for me the side effects of my treatment are mostly menopausal. 'Brain Fog' mostly.

There has been a total body change; I'm not a 30 inch around my chest anymore! A stone and a half heavier. No Boobs. I am a really weird shape. My physical confidence is really low.

Then there is a loss of libido, anxiety, sleeping can be an issue, hot flushes, and mentally I find it even more difficult.

I still keep fit and exercise, I meditate daily, I have a vegetarian diet and I hold the ones I love very close. "While I can, I will" is my mantra for where I am with everything. My side effects are do-able, but I do stumble and fall, and it seems with every cycle I take, it gets a bit harder.

As the bubble of Covid popped and we all started emerging into life, I felt lost and lonely. I was adapting to living with cancer. I started looking around for people who might get what I was going through. I started a bit of an Instagram life, and had reached out many times to 'Make Seconds Count'. So, when they came down to Brighton to do an event with some of the ladies from 'Loose Women', I volunteered.

I got to meet Lisa who was the founder of the charity. Lisa said 'Oh, by the way, we've got an event coming up in Liverpool and somebody dropped out would you like to be part of a photo shoot?' Yeah, it sounds great, OK. I had one friend who had the same diagnosis as me and I had started to connect with people on social media; however this was the first time I was going to meet people face to face.

It was also a chance to gain confidence with my new body. I had chosen to have another mastectomy. The udder had to go and although reconstruction surgery was a thing, the thought of such a massive operation didn't appeal. I thought I would need my strength at a later date. So, to be more equal I had my other boob removed. They were never twins my boobs, but even now the two sides are so different, more like sisters. However, I was so much happier flat.

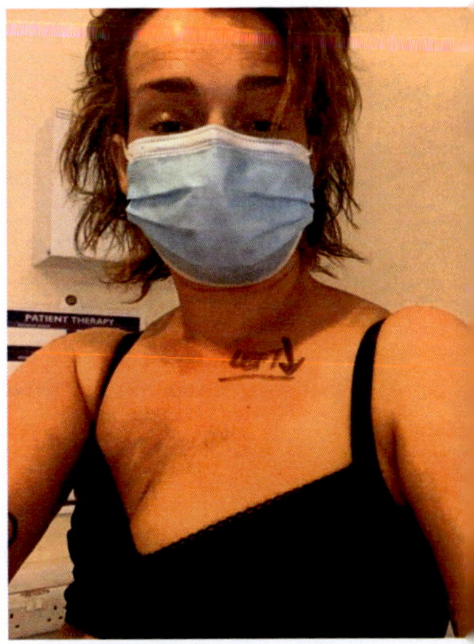

Going up to Liverpool on my own was a

really big deal. I met with Jeannie before from Instagram; neither of us wanted to walk in alone. So, it was easy just chatting away, an instant connection, a bond. Walking up together made a real difference. I didn't know what to expect about the whole thing. I was hoping for a bit more glamour, so was disappointed when we were told to bring black leggings and a black long sleeve top. Especially now I was flat, well, more concaved.

On arriving at the boxing ring the first person to meet me was Sally; she gave me the biggest hug. I think she just needed something to hold on to, and that was my introduction to this new community. I had found it was just funny; it was funny being there; it was funny being there knowing people you've not spoken to, but you knew because you had seen them on Instagram. There was a lot of laughter. This was my tribe, people I had met, hugged, looked in their eyes. All of us were really out of our comfort zones, but sharing this amazing experience.

The main image created, and the photoshoot itself, was really empowering (even in black leggings!). I was moved from the back, to the front, to the side; can we try you here? In the end I was towards the back, in fact on most reproductions of the image you can't see me at all.

However, in the moment with those people, in those photos, and I suppose with all that makeup and positive attention, I actually felt strong, brave and beautiful. For the first time in a long time. It was a very special day, with a very strong message. I had found my tribe and this was only the start of the story.

What a thrill it was when I saw myself twice on that billboard; well, not really twice because as I said I wasn't really on it; I was on the side, but twice on billboards nonetheless. I saw them once, whilst on holiday, and once in my local shopping centre in Brighton. More importantly our message was out there.

Very quickly things started to change within the group; that amazing day became a distant memory as the reality of the disease took hold. We lost 4 members so quickly one after the other. This led the group to become a charity. I can't take any credit for this. However, this is a group of strong, passionate, courageous women, and there was no stopping them wanting to make a difference, and for the plight of secondary breast cancer patients to be heard.

2023 was when the gang were all together again. It was charity launch day! This time we didn't have to wear black leggings and black shirt. This time we got dolled up; we got dolled up good and proper and we're going to be launching the charity "Fighting to be Heard" on "The Real Housewives of Chester". It was my Mum's birthday too, so I invited her along to be part of it.

We were spoilt rotten; it was the launch of the charity, so we had our hair styled, we were given outfits to wear. We were asked to talk about our stories and about this incredible group of women. I had a rough plan in my head during the rehearsal but hadn't written anything down. By the time it was time to do it for real I was a little bit drunk.

I do remember that I said that this group of women were like a bungee cord, because when you get a secondary diagnosis, it feels like you have been pushed off a cliff. All your hope and dreams are taken away, and you feel like you are free falling; but before I hit the bottom, these women were around me and pulled me back up.

The last time I saw many of them was for the Charity Ball. I did a bit of compering and helped host the event. It was super special to see lots of the girls there, and we raised lots of money; which gave us another excuse to get dressed up!

It is a privilege to be part of this group. So many of them have inspired me, pushed me further, made me think differently, they are incredible.

We are “Fighting to be Heard”
I am fighting too.

If one in two of us will get cancer, shouldn’t that be the go-to check? ‘It might be cancer, let’s rule it out first.’

Training for oncologists on how to talk about a secondary diagnosis. Words are key; let’s not talk dates, averages and life span.

Full body scans for both primary patients and secondary.

Compulsory mammograms from an earlier age. 50 is too old.

Have quicker response times for scans.

CHAPTER 22

EMILY ROBERTS

My girl, my life, my everything, my daughter Emily.

That's how I started her eulogy. Never for one moment did I think that day would come. I would never let that thought enter my head; I wasn't going to lose my loud, gobby, bossy, beautiful girl. But I did, and there are no words to describe the pain.

Two years ago, in February 2022, her consultant called us to report that the latest scan results were positive: her stage 4 diagnosis was stable, and treatment was working amazingly well. So, we booked a trip to Lapland in December for her three little girls, Isla (9), Edie (5), and Anni (3): something to look forward to and make memories. Emily's wish was for her girls to meet Santa. A week later, on 7 February 2022, with no warning, she was gone; in a matter of hours, I lost my beautiful daughter.

If I can be thankful for anything, it is that I found her, she saw me, she knew I was there. I was able to get her brother, dad, stepdad and partner to the hospital. She wasn't alone, she wasn't aware, she wasn't in pain; she went peacefully.

This awful chapter of her illness began in June 2020 at the age of 28. Three weeks after her primary diagnosis of breast cancer, she was given her second diagnosis, as five spots were found on her liver. One year later, in June 2021, it had progressed to her spine; then, in October, lymph nodes were affected. She was now stage 4 - not curable but hopefully manageable. She didn't want to know how many years she possibly had; she believed she was going to be here forever (the doctors estimated 3–5 years). To the doctors' amazement she fought sepsis and Covid twice. Unknown to anyone, it had spread to her brain and without any warning she suffered a bleed; the consultant's words were: "She's not going to survive this."

Throughout her illness, she continued to do acts of kindness, charity work and fundraising of all sorts. She was passionate about raising awareness of this awful disease, sharing her story on her Facebook page and reaching out to other women going through the same experience. Even though she was stage 4 (not curable but manageable), she helped support ladies, even with a better diagnosis, getting together a little group of locals to meet up and socialise, which is still ongoing.

Emily joined Fighting2BeHeard in its first year and appeared on their first campaign; this powerful image is still being used. These ladies are "Fighting to be Heard," campaigning for more regular tests and scans. If Emily had been given more regular brain scans, maybe she would still be here maybe not. She loved being part of this gang, sadly for a short time, as she was the first one to pass, and now the image shows her faded out along with six others. When I saw this, it absolutely broke me, but that's the point another powerful message for the charity. I am so grateful to them for still including my girl in their campaigns, and I know she would be thrilled; she always wanted to be, and usually was, the centre of attention.

Emily was the most amazing daughter, sister, friend and the best mummy ever; she gave so much love to everyone she met. Her language was colourful; she was loud and gobby, you knew when she entered the room (even as a child). She loved to spoil people, especially me… and oh, I miss that so much. We went everywhere together; she always chose me. We were besties, not a day went by without talking, seeing or FaceTiming. Although I'm surrounded by friends, I feel so lost and lonely without her. Everyone who saw or met her commented on what an amazing, fun-loving mummy she was; her girls came first every time, through everything even on bad days they were her priority. They were so loved, and they knew it.

I asked her girls if they could talk to her or write a letter, what would they say?

Isla, now aged 12: To Mummy, I wish you were still here with us to cuddle and comfort us when we feel sad (your hugs were the best). I miss you a lot, and so does everyone else. I hope wherever you are, you are happy and not in pain or sad. Love you to the moon and back and back again.

Edie, now aged 7: Hope you're doing OK up in heaven and you're playing with Poppy (our old dog), Cinderella (her old pet rat) and Pascalle (pet chameleon).

Anni, now aged 5: I love you. I've made meatballs for tea and baked cakes with Nanny. My favourite colours are pink and white... It's the same colour as Mummy's angel wings. If I could wave a wand, I'd say, "Mummy, come back."

So, what now? Well, we all carry on; we all get up and do our day for each other, her friends, her girls, but more importantly, for her. We all carry her with us, talk about her and continue to support her charities. We all look after, guide, love and support her girlies, and tell them all about their amazing mummy. We plan to continue holding an Emfest charity event each year to raise awareness, to remember and honour her.

We've planted trees in our field for her and will hopefully add more every year for Christmas and her birthdays. Her ashes are scattered there around a summerhouse which looks over the Shropshire countryside, a beautiful place for us to sit and spend time with the most beautiful girl. We may not be able to see her, but she's here with us every day, and when I see her again, I hope she will say, "Hey Mum, you did well; I'm proud of you," just as I am the proudest mummy to her. Oh, and I will absolutely fulfil my girl's wishes for her girlies to meet Santa in Lapland.

I say again: my girl, my life, my everything, my daughter Emily.

I hope our story brings attention to the fact that more action is desperately needed: more regular full-body MRI scans, as we all know, this awful disease spreads to every part of the body. It had spread to my girl's brain, and we were totally unaware. As her mum, I obviously go to the very dark thoughts of "if only, maybe, if we had known," which is absolutely heartbreaking; I have to pull myself out of those thoughts, otherwise I would go under.

To everyone and anyone reading this... get the word out there.

In Loving Memory

07.02.2022

CHAPTER 23

HELENA AWUAKYE

Dear reader, my name is Helena Awuakye, and I want to share my story to hopefully give hope to others going through this journey.

Before I embark on my journey with cancer, let me tell you a little about myself.

I was born in London in 1975. Both my parents are Ghanaian. When I was three years old, I went to live in Ghana. I was blessed to spend five years there, and I returned to the UK when I was eight. I grew up in Camden Town, London.

At the age of eighteen, I left London to attend Manchester University, where I studied Dentistry. My time in Manchester was one of the best of my life. I made lifelong friends, who have supported me through many difficult times.

Student life was great, and after I qualified, I gave birth to my little bundle of joy, Josh. I moved back to London for his birth, and when a job opportunity arose, I decided to move to South Wales. I initially took the job as a locum, with every intention of moving back to London after three months. However, twenty years later I am still in South Wales. It's where Josh calls home.

Life in Wales was normal. As a single mum, life came with its challenges, but nothing I couldn't handle. My job as a dentist was stressful at times, but very rewarding. I worked in the same dental practice for eighteen years. I loved my job, and I loved my patients. I could never have imagined leaving dentistry. I was committed to it and could never have imagined doing anything else.

Overall, I thought I was very healthy. I had never had any serious illnesses. I kept fit and ate a relatively healthy diet. My sister had been diagnosed with leukaemia at the age of twenty-five, thirteen years ago. I remembered one of the doctors at the time saying that she had survived her gruelling treatment because she was young and had a strong heart. Well, I wasn't young, but I thought: 'I'm going to do everything I can to keep my heart strong.' From that time, I was committed to keeping fit.

I started with running, which was difficult at first, but went on to complete several 5ks, 10ks and three half marathons for charity. In fact, my first half marathon was to raise money for Velindre Cancer Hospital, which is where I now have my treatment. Alongside the running, I also did strength training, HIIT and mobility exercises.

Working out was my way of de-stressing at the end of a challenging day. It kept me mentally sane, and I loved it.

Alongside my workouts and healthy eating, my faith gave me strength, peace, and joy. I have been brought up as a Christian my whole life, and whilst I have not always walked with God, I know He has always walked with me. Every challenging season of my life, I know He has been there. He is my source of strength.

When my sister was critically ill, I felt reassurance from God that all would be well, even though we were told to expect the worst. My sister pulled through against all the odds. She inspires me every day.

So, lets fast forward to 2021. We are all living in the pandemic and life has been stressful for everyone. I found it particularly stressful working as a dentist during the pandemic. Life was fast paced and constantly changing. Working in PPE that we could never have imagined, but somehow, we coped. We were one of the first to be offered the vaccine. I took everything in my stride and generally thought that I had coped well with everything.

I can't say for sure how long the lump in my right breast had been present. I had been aware of it for a while but thought it would go away. I had discovered a lump many years ago, which I had had checked. I was reassured that it was nothing, and eventually it went away. I just thought this would be the same, but after a while I realised that it wasn't going away. If anything, it was getting bigger and harder. I still wasn't concerned. Afterall I was healthy and fit so it couldn't be anything sinister, could it?

I finally decided to ring the GP to get it checked. Due to the pandemic I had to have a phone consultation first, which I had the same day I contacted the GP. I had a face-to-face consultation the following day. I wasn't concerned, and so I only told my practice manager as I need time off work and one other person. I didn't tell my family or any of my friends. I didn't want to worry them, and I honestly thought it was going to be nothing.

At the face-to-face appointment the GP was concerned. She told me she was going to do a cancer referral, as she could also feel the lymph nodes in my armpits on that side. She told me that I should be seen within two and a half weeks, but due to covid it could take up to three. I remember walking to my car, and for the first time I felt scared. I went back to work as normal and carried on with my list of patients for the day. The anxiety eased off over the next few weeks, as I told myself there couldn't be anything wrong.

Two and a half weeks later I was seen at my local hospital, where I had a consultation, a mammogram, an ultrasound and a biopsy, all on the same day. Due to covid, I had to attend the appointment on my own. I was given an appointment six days later to get my results.

I literally felt like I was in a dream, or should I say nightmare. I just couldn't believe what was happening. I just kept on thinking surely, all this will be for nothing, it's going to be ok.

My sister was coming to stay with me from London the week of my results, so I was forced to tell her what was going on. That week just seemed to drag. It was the longest week of my life. I worked the morning of my appointment, finished work and drove home to pick up my sister. All the way there she encouraged me to stay positive, and in my head, I was telling myself the same.

When we got to the hospital there was a little wait before I was called in for my results. We were called into the room by the breast care nurse. Before the consultant opened his mouth to say anything, I knew the results weren't good. His face said it all. I heard something like 'I'm sorry you have cancer' and the rest became a bit of a blur. A rough outline of treatment was discussed, and I was told that I would need to take a year off work. To which I replied 'I can't, what about my patients'. My initial treatment plan consisted of chemotherapy to shrink the tumour, followed by surgery and radiotherapy.

I wasn't really taking anything in. My sister did a good job asking all the questions, I'm so glad she was with me. It felt like the rug had been pulled from under neath me and I was just free falling. I can't remember if I cried in that consultation room, but as soon as I stepped out the flood gates opened. My sister just held me, and we both cried. She told me I was going to be alright. I tried to think positively, but I was also scared. I just couldn't understand how this had happened. I did all the right things. I ate well, exercised, so why me. But why not me. No one deserves to get cancer. It is not ageist, sexist or racist. It simply does not discriminate.

The next few days that followed were some of the hardest days during this journey. My sister and I went to have some food after the appointment whilst I figured out how to tell my son. He was at work, so I called him to come home straight after he finished. He sensed something was wrong and insisted I tell him what was going on. I couldn't tell him over the phone so, I drove to his work, and he came to meet me in the car. It was the most heartbreaking thing I've had to do. I told him and we both just cried. My biggest fear was leaving him. He always used to say, 'It's you and me against the world Mum'. This just seemed so unfair.

I proceeded to tell my parents, my siblings and my friends. Over the next few days, each conversation brought a fresh wave of tears. I was just so drained. I was worried how my Dad would cope. He had already been through this with my sister. Surprisingly he was fine, and I was relieved. He just encouraged me to stay positive.

Throughout my treatment I received so much love, support and encouragement. I was overwhelmed. I'm not the sort of person that readily accepts help, but through this I accepted whatever help was offered. My son, family, friends, neighbours, church family, work colleagues and my patients were amazing. I couldn't have been better supported.

The next few weeks were filled with various scan appointments, and blood tests. I also had a breast clip placed so that they could locate the original site of the tumour. This became irritated and I needed a course of antibiotics to settle it down.

After all the scans I was diagnosed with stage three breast cancer aged forty-six. It was oestrogen positive, Her 2 positive and progesterone negative. It had spread to the lymph nodes in my arm pit, and a CT scan had picked up an area on my liver which needed further investigation. If this was cancer, then it would mean I had secondary breast cancer.

I quietly started to prepare for the treatment ahead. I decided to keep working until two weeks before I started treatment. I decided to cut my hair really short rather than see clumps of hair fall out.

My first chemotherapy was started six weeks after I was told my initial results. That morning, I prayed to God to give me the strength to go through the treatment. And before I left to go to the hospital I prayed with Josh and my sister. I felt relatively calm as one of my best friends drove me to my first appointment. We both shed tears as we said our goodbyes. I was scared walking into the ward on my own, but I had no choice I had to get this done.

The first round of chemotherapy was Epirubicin and cyclophosphamide. I had decided to cold cap, so this made the appointment time even longer. Having afro hair also meant additional time. Overall, my first chemo round was fine, and I was super proud that I had managed to get through it on my own. The nurses who looked after me were amazing at each appointment. They were gentle, kind and reassuring. I'm not the best patient, and I'm not very good with needles but with their reassurance I managed to get through each appointment. I am eternally grateful to all the doctors and nurses who have been involved in my care.

Three weeks after I had my first chemotherapy it was confirmed that there was metastatic spread to the liver. Surprisingly I wasn't too freaked out. I guess I had known from the beginning that, that could be the case. I was told that I would receive Docetaxel and targeted therapy at the next round and going forward.

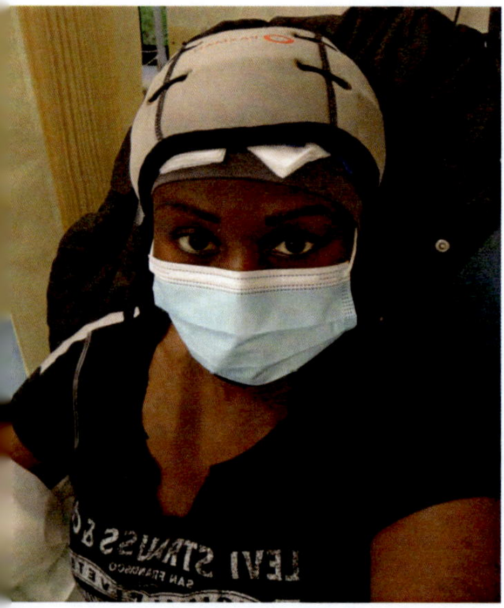

Chemotherapy was no walk in the park. It was tough, and I coped with it as best as I could. For me prayer and exercise were my go-to. My church family supported me in prayer. I was able to keep on exercising through my treatment, although towards the end I was only able to manage long walks. I was just grateful to be able to keep moving. On the days I felt tired I just rested.

During the treatment I had some of the side effects that I was warned about. I lost some of my hair, but it started to grow back before I finished the chemo. My nails turned black, and although the discoloration has gone, my nails are very thin and brittle. Thankfully

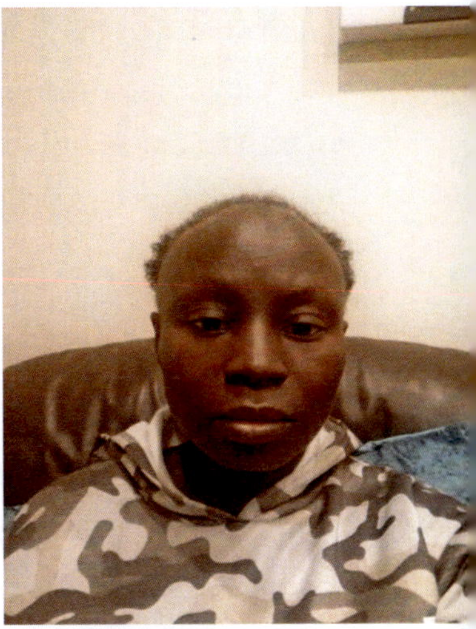

I didn't suffer with nausea. As the rounds of chemo went by, I began to feel fatigued. This I found difficult as I just liked to be able to do things. The other side effect I struggled with was loss of my taste sensation. This would generally happen a few days after chemo, and just when my taste sensation was returning, I would be hit with the next round. One of the hardest side effects I struggled with, and still struggle with is neuropathy of my fingers and toes. I have a constant sensation of pins and needles. On a day-to-day basis I can function and do everything, but the neuropathy has robbed me of a job that I loved dearly.

Unfortunately, the chemotherapy put me in a medically induced menopause, which brought on extreme hot flushes and night sweats. I am still battling with them, but they have eased a little in the last few weeks.

After seven rounds of chemo, the chemo treatment finished in January 2022. I was glad to see the back of that phase of treatment, the targeted drug therapy carries on.

Whilst undergoing treatment, sadly my stepmum was diagnosed with cancer and she later passed away. No matter how positive you try to be, loosing someone to cancer when you are going through it yourself hits you hard. For a while it triggered my fear, but I had to remind myself that everyone's journey is different.

Once chemo was done, I started to get back to my new normal.

I had shielded the whole time I was having treatment, so slowly I started to see my friends again. My family had been great, taking it in turn to come down from London to look after me so that my son wouldn't feel overwhelmed. Now it was time to start living again.

Towards the end of my treatment, I decided to make some changes. It was triggered by a saying by Chris wark 'You can't heal in the same environment that cancer was created'. I wanted to take control of how I could help myself. The changes I made were centred around eliminating toxins, whether it was toxins I was eating, drinking, putting on my skin or emotional toxins.

During my treatment I made a difficult decision to tackle a strained relationship with a close loved one. I was feeling hurt and let down. It was a constant pain in my heart I just could not shake. The hurt I was feeling was eating me up inside. I wanted to be free of this negative emotion. I decided to write how I was feeling in a letter. As hard as it was, it was the best thing I did. It gave as the opportunity to sit and talk openly. It allowed me to forgive, and with that I felt like a weight had been lifted off my shoulder. I learnt there is freedom and power in the act of forgiveness.

I changed my diet to an organic whole food, plant-based diet. I incorporated fresh cold pressed juices. I changed my makeup and personal hygiene products making sure they did not contain any parabens, sodium laurel sulphate, formaldehyde, phthalates or synthetic fragrances that could increase oestrogen levels. I replaced all plastic bottles and containers with glass. Oh, and I also gave up alcohol!

Alongside these changes I kept up with my fitness and six months after finishing the chemo treatment I was able to take part in a Race for life 5k supported by family and friends. It was a sign that I could still do things I enjoyed doing. And a few weeks ago, I took part in the 10k winter race.

My faith also kept on growing, and on May 22nd, 2022, I was baptised. I have managed to find peace and joy on this journey, and that's what my faith brings me. A scripture verse I quote daily ' I will not die , but live and proclaim what the Lord has done' gives me peace when I have my not so good days.

So, life continued to coast along steadily. Some of the side effects from treatment became more tolerable. I started to connect with other women who were on this cancer journey. A friend of mine introduced me to black women rising charity. I became a member and joined one of the support groups, living with cancer. The meetings take place via zoom. I was a little nervous, but the ladies soon put me at ease. I still take part in the zoom meetings. It's a great space to talk about what's happening in our lives, cancer and non-cancer related. We have a chat and a good laugh.

It was nice to be able to connect with other black women who have the same or similar experience to what I was going through. I feel the black community are reluctant to talk about subjects like cancer. Black women rising do an amazing job getting awareness into the black community and giving support.

Through Black women rising, I was connected to the fighting to be heard foundation. I was told it was a new charity that was launching.

It's aim, to provide financial and emotional support for those living with secondary breast cancer and their families. What an amazing ethos. Living with secondary breast cancer comes with so many challenges. This can affect your ability to work and earn. So being able to give financial support, and help families live or make special memories, just made so much sense. I also wanted other black women feel that it was a foundation they could approach.

I was asked to take part in a photo shoot for international women's day. I made my way to Manchester from Newport. Needless to say, I was nervous, I didn't know what to expect. The moment I walked into the studio; I was made to feel so welcome. All the ladies knew each other from the original fighting to be heard campaign, so I was the newbie.

We had an amazing day having our makeup done and wearing gorgeous outfits from Forever unique, then posing for our individual and group photos. I got to know the back story of how the ladies had come together. They were an amazing group of women, and I was moved by how they had come together. I was told that Seema from the real housewives of cheshire would be joining us. I learnt how she had become involved in the charity. The day just represented a group of women coming together and empowering one another.

I walked away feeling I had made friends, so when I was asked to be a part of the launch and fashion show, it was a no brainer. I said yes! I was due to have treatment the day of the launch, but my consultant kindly rescheduled it so I could take part.

Making my way to Manchester again I was filled with anxiety and excitement. I was nervous about standing up and telling my story to people I didn't know. Although I was out of my comfort zone, I felt it was important to push through my anxiety. It was important that we share our stories.

What can I say, the launch day was epic. We were pampered and made to feel like queens. We laughed, we ate, some drank, we danced, but most importantly we shared our stories so that we could be heard.

No body wants a cancer diagnosis, and it has changed my life dramatically. Some negative changes but also a lot of positive changes. It's the community no one wants to be a part of, but I have met some amazing and inspirational people along the way.

I am living my best life. I am being kind to myself and living at a slower pace of life. I have incorporated strategies to help detox and cope with stress. So instead of juggling life at one hundred miles an hour, I have slowed it right down, I am grateful for every day, every experience every moment I spend with family and friends. I have experienced humanity at its kindest, and most loving and I have been deeply moved. I have taken the time to travel, which I wouldn't have done before.

I refuse to live in fear, but instead chose to live in hope. And that's my wish , that being a part of this book will give others hope. There is life with secondary breast cancer, its just a different life, and that's ok.

CHAPTER 24

VICKY KEATING

Written by Debbie, Vickys Mum

My daughter Vicki was the bravest, most overpoweringly inspiring person that I have ever known. Headstrong as they come, she confronted her illness with a fire and ferocity that could not help but galvanise those around her. Her energy was relentless, her personality infectious. She never wavered at being a devoted mother, daughter, sister, partner or friend during even the harshest days of her treatment.

From day one Vicki made a promise to herself to document her cancer journey through her Facebook blog "Tales of the Triple Negative Boobie", with the intention of educating and inspiring women in her position who were seeking reassurance that they were not alone, or seeking comfort through shared experience. It says it all that, aged just 28, her first thought was to turn a negative situation into a positive one, using her experience for the good of others. I am so, so proud of her.

If Vicki were here today she would be found beside her children Grayson and Rey, laughing, playing, loving them as only a mother can. She would say that nobody "fights" cancer. It is an illness that simply does not care how tough you are, and Vicki was as tough as they come. All you can do is make as many memories as you can, live for the moment, reach out to the community if you are struggling and never, never give up.

Through the memories she made with those she loved, and now through this book, my beautiful Vicki lives on, shining just as bright as the day she blessed my life on 23 June 1990.

I love and miss her so very much.

In Loving Memory

31.08.2022

CHAPTER 25

NATALIE EDWARDS-WHITE

Hyper focusing Cancer

Type of Breast Cancer: ER+, PR+, Her2 Low

Hi, I'm Natalie, 40, and I'm mum to two incredible boys, George (12) and Henry (11). Despite having Secondary Breast Cancer, I still work full time and I am a Social Sustainability & Wellbeing Manager in the Construction/facilities Industry. I like cats, Christmas, travel, alternative treatments (alongside conventional of course) and I hate hotpot and corned beef hash! I have an insane long-term memory which I pride myself on (although others find it extremely annoying at times) I am a fountain of all knowledge due to my ability to hyperfocus and fixate. This is both a positive and a Negative!

Cancer has taught me many valuable lessons over the past 7 years: how to live, how to learn, how to advocate for myself, how to set boundaries, how to support myself through diet, nutrition, integrative practices and how important it is to look after my own Mental Health and Well-being above everything else!

My Cancer Journey over the past 7 years has not always been plain sailing. I have had massive highs for 3 years, and then 2023 was a year of 2 progressions, the death of my beloved Dad to a quick onset of Motor Neurone Disease and a rapid decline in Health, which saw me not being treated week after week. 2023 was the year I didn't look after myself physically, mentally, nutritionally, and everything else in between. And what a massive wakeup call October 2023 was!

I was 33 when I was diagnosed with primary Breast Cancer. I'd unfortunately been back and too to the GP with a Lump in my right breast. I was told on two occasions it was Mastitis. 'Well, that's a bit unusual I thought, I haven't breast fed in over 3 years' – By the 3rd visit and after two rounds of antibiotics, something was niggling, so I took myself private and low and behold on March 15th 2019 I was told I had an early-stage Breast Cancer. My boys were 4 and 5.

2 Surgeries, 6 rounds of Chemo, 15 rounds of Radiotherapy and no eyebrows and eyelashes later I was sent on my way with a prescription of Tamoxifen. Never scanned. I had no lymph node involvement, so I was deemed low risk and fine. I should note here that I made it clear at the time of my surgery that I had some leg and hip pain which funnily went away with chemo. (This was obviously secondaries looking back)

Unfortunately, a few months later we were hit by a global pandemic and my first 6 monthly scan was cancelled in the march. I'd started getting pains in my left hip that were getting worse and by April I was sitting on ergonomic cushions to support the pain with me working from home. Obviously, this was a period where everyone was working from home and musculoskeletal problems were arising. My pain was explained by my team. I felt relieved and that it was more than likely the Tamoxifen. My oncologist was on Maternity leave So I had been liaising weekly about the pain with different members of my then team. By August (and still not seen or been told to go to A&E) I took myself off to a chiropractor who sent my X-Rays to a colleague. They told me there was something going

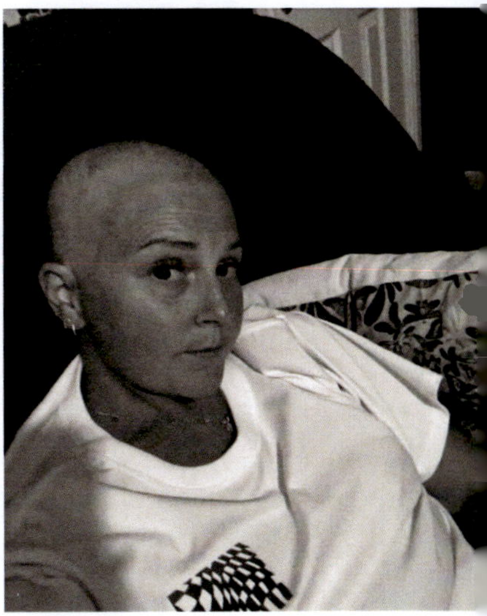

on in my pelvic area and although they were not saying it was Cancer - they were saying I had bone loss. I sent them to my GP who had forwarded onto my Team. Nobody looked at my X-Rays for 6 weeks despite me chasing. When they were looked at, I was told 'They look fine'. Now I appreciate everyone was in unchartered territory BUT this was not ok. This was pure neglect in every way, shape and form. By the time I finally got a Scan, it was November 12th 2020. I had been using crutches for 6 weeks; I was crawling across the floor with the washing basket as I could barely pull myself up due to the pain. At 6.00pm that same night I received a call from a member of the Team I had been speaking to for the past 4 months to tell me I had Secondary Breast Cancer in my bones and Lungs, that I had a few months left to live! And above all, my left femur was completely broken at the head. I also had multiple pelvic fractures and a fracture to my T11. (That explained the pain and why I couldn't walk) Imagine being told that whilst you were dishing out the turkey dinosaurs!!

I was rushed into Whiston Hospital for an emergency hip replacement. In anger through gritted teeth, I told the person at the end of the phone that they had told me there was nothing wrong and that my X-Rays were fine. That person apologised and explained she had been lying awake the night before, wondering what they could and should have done. The next day, I changed my care to a fantastic Oncologist and Team at Whiston and St Helens Lilac Centre, where I remained for over 3 years.

I'm a firm believer that negativity attracts negativity, 'The law of attraction' – Let's set the scene .....you're having a bad day, your late for work because you lost your car keys, your stressed, you get stopped at every red light going, you spill your coffee, you miss a meeting. Everything follows a pattern. You let negativity in and it destroys you from the inside out! I have literally seen this happen! I decided whilst lay in my hospital bed that I wasn't going to let this affect me negatively, I was not going to go through years of fighting and lodging a complaint through the system and instructing legal teams. I was going to move forward. It was difficult at times, and I most definitely have had some Trauma counselling post the 2020 event. (which I highly recommend)

But something that I need to say here(and as I type this, I can feel the weight lifting off of me).... I want that individual to know that I forgive their mistake and the medical neglect I experienced, and that's the first time I have been able to say that since 2020.

I'd been relatively disciplined in the mindset area until 2023. I welcomed in absolute chaos and stress through grief, worry, anxiety through what was happening to my Dad and then his untimely death. October 23 saw me have progression to my liver for the second time that year. I had to go back onto IV Chemotherapy – Paclitaxol ...weekly and immediately. My Team were and still are fantastic, but unfortunately my bloods were not playing ball and due to NHS protocol, I was not being treated. But how could I get the cancer under control if I couldn't get the treatment inside me because both Cancer and the Chemo were affecting how my Haemoglobin and platelets were produced? This is what happens with bone mets and subsequently bone marrow infiltration. Why is the protocol for blood cancer different? You can literally take your entire immune system offline! It's still cancer at the end of the day and they are allowed to be treated on low everything to kill their cancer....why should we be any different? I felt myself getting sicker. I was on weekly blood transfusions at this point, and I struggled to make it up the stairs without getting breathless from the anaemia.

I always said that when it was time to pull my Private Healthcare out of my back pocket, I would, and I did just that one Wednesday Morning in early November 2023. I'm so grateful that I have this. I know not everyone does, I know I'm incredibly lucky and believe me when I say, I am grateful every day for this. I felt incredibly guilty regarding the Private element. As I wasn't using it, I didn't tell people I had it. But at the end of the day, this is a benefit me and my family have and it's my life line now.

There is a clear difference between Private Care and NHS care regardless of what people say. It's not about the nicer lunches and more comfortable settings.... It's a difference between additional genetic testing, getting your foundation one covered, it's a difference between access to more Life saving drugs that are approved by the European Medical Agencies but not NICE and the NHS. It's a difference between quicker access to Scan's and tests and it's a difference between being able to be treated the way your consultant wants to treat you. Everywhere has guidelines and protocols, I understand that – they are mostly there to keep us safe but there are circumstances where you need to be treated based on your overall clinical stability.

In April 2024 I had an overall 'Stable scan' after 6 months on

Paclitaxel but my CA153 Tumour marker was rising and there was an inconclusive area in my liver. We upped my chemo for another 8 weeks and in June 2024 it was clear it was more growth in my liver. We did a Foundation 1 liquid biopsy and 3 weeks later, It was confirmed I have the ESR1 Mutation. A new drug Elacestrant (Korserdu) had been approved by the FDA and European medicines agency the previous year, and had attained it's UK license in Feb 24. This meant I was able to access this drug through private medical as it isn't available on the NHS. I stayed on this drug for 8 weeks before my CA153 went wild! As I was the first person in the whole of Clatterbridge to get this drug, it wasn't safe to keep me on it with not enough supporting evidence and my person opinion is – it's not good enough as a drug on it's own. There are trials currently alongside the 'Ciclib' drugs. A note though here, we could kind of pin point which areas of my liver had the ESR1 mutation as they 'shrunk significantly' on this drug.

I have an incredible support network at home, but I realised quite early on in my secondary diagnosis that I was struggling with not having someone to talk to from within the Cancer Community who 'got it'; someone I could form a friendship with and to feel less alone. For this reason, I applied for a charity photo shoot that I saw advertised on a Support Facebook group. This was the start of 20 Ladies coming together' Fighting to be heard'. I'm still to this day not quite sure why I applied – Things like this are massively out of my comfort zone! I mean, you've probably guessed it already from my ramblings.... I'm AuDHD (Autism and Inattentive ADHD) and so my neurodivergent brain doesn't think the same as a neurotypical person, nor does it process the same. Anything social like this is super awkward for me and in turn makes my skin crawl with anxiety and awkwardness. Funny really as when at work, I can stand up in a room full of people and deliver a talk or training with no problem whatsoever. I've learnt to mask in situations over the years, read people's energy, try and mimic elements of their personality as to make myself more appealing in social situations. Unfortunately, it will often end up with me retreating and feeling even more uncomfortable so a lot of the time I say no to things. It can just be easier. Some people's energy will always be a little bit too much for me but that's not on them, it's me and how that makes me feel and I've learnt that this is ok. My feelings are most definitely valid and I know I do better in smaller social situations where I can be myself. I met a lot of incredible women that day, from those volunteering their time and specialist skillsets, to all the women who had/have Secondary Breast Cancer. I learnt very quickly that a lot of these women had been living already for years with the disease AND more importantly.....doing well. I came away from the day with a massive boost of positivity, and the group WhatsApp we had was invaluable in that first year. Unfortunately, 5 of our Ladies passed away in the year following the shoot in very close proximity to each other, and the WhatsApp group became a very heavy place to be. I know others would have felt the same, but I personally couldn't cope with seeing this heartache on a day to day basis. Children losing their mums, Husbands loosing their wives, people suffering. It was overwhelming. With my Dad falling sick too, it was time for me to leave the group. I'm forever grateful for Lisa Fleming and Kate Orr for bringing us together on that day.

For me integrative practices, mindfulness and research are extremely important to me. The first thing I did in November was ask my new oncologist how he felt about me supplementing, using Hyberbaric Oxygen Therapy and switching out my water to an ionised Alkaline Kangen Water Machine. He was open, he listened, he talked and agreed that I should invest in a decent pre and probiotic because of the link between gut health and the immune system. It was like music to my ears. I'd felt incredibly guilty about leaving my old team up until this point but this cemented my decision.

I could sit here and harp on about research I've done over the past 5 years, books I've read, practices I have tried but we will always be met with a mix of opinions on this topic. I personally know stress and trauma was the root of the Cancer (plenty of research on the link between hormonal Breast cancers and stress – Again – My belief) and I know that when my diet, supplementation, exercise, mental health has been disciplined and good – the cancer has been stable. Make what you like of that....I have multiple medical professionals involved in my care whom are all subject matter experts in their areas and I have an enormous amount of respect for them – You know who you are - Thank you.

In June 2025, it was time for me to access 'Enhertu' – A hugely controversial subject as I'm HER2 low and this is currently available in England and Wales for my breast cancer. I have a friend funding for her life. At £10K every 3 weeks, it's not cheap but the data is there! I'm grateful I have it; I feel guilty for those that don't and inequality in healthcare is 100% NOT ok. This shouldn't be happening in 2025.

Advice

1. If I had any advise to give to non- Cancer patients reading this it would be....Get your insurances sorted, life insurance, critical illness, Private medical. It becomes invaluable when you have a disease such as this and you will be thankful to younger you if that time came about! It's minimal money to pay when you are classed as fit and healthy. When you are in a situation like mine, private medical can open you up to so many more doors treatment wise. It is literally a matter of your life. Don't be complacent as to think 'This will never happen to me' . I used to think that way. NOTE: Inequality and postcode lotteries are not ok in healthcare!

2. Secondly for those newly diagnosed....it's ok to not want to be visible in Cancer Land all the time. Of course it's fantastic to have people you can relate to whom are going through similar to you, but know and notice when it is becoming too much and do something about it. Follow the accounts on Instagram, join the Facebook groups – but mute/restrict them If it becomes too much. I do. The Law of attraction again, if you are seeing negativity – guess what? Yep, you got it! Send your friends a text to let them know you are thinking of them, like their posts from time to time BUT protect yourself and your own mental health and wellbeing. It does not make you a bad person by doing this. I do not feel bad for not being In the majority of WhatsApp groups. I'm proud of myself for setting those boundaries for myself. The old me wasn't as disciplined in that area.

3. Thirdly, your Journey is your journey and it should not be compared to someone else's! Just because you have the same type of breast cancer as your friend, it does not mean that your treatment line is going to fail because theirs did. We all have different genetic

makeups, different mutations (and I'm not talking about the ones we are allowed to test for on the NHS). No two stories are the same! Remember that. It's critical to changing your thought process.

4. Invest in the Foundation 1/Guardant 360 Liquid Biopsy test. Mine came back to show I have an ESR1 mutation.

5. Diet, nutrition, mindfulness, exercise and integrative practices are great 'support' alongside conventional oncology. Do the research yourself (if you want to – I'm not a medical professional and most definitely would not be advising this be done without oncology). Targeted Therapies, Immunotherapies, and Chemotherapies are fantastic for slowing tumours down in their tracks – sometimes getting rid of them altogether. (You wouldn't see me moving away from these approaches) But they don't get rid of Cancer Stem cells. Everything else will help support your body and keep it strong and healthy. Look into Supplementation with a nutritionist's support, exercise, go to Sound Bath's and Reflexology and if you have the spare funds to look into PEMF, Hyperbaric oxygen therapy (HBOT) and Alkaline Water to name but a few. There are lots of charity's out there whom can support with some of the above practices. See what's available in your local community.

6. Therapy! Get to the bottom of your stress. Support your Mental Health. CBT, Trauma counselling, or medication if need be.

7. Never EVER let someone give you a prognosis! It is the most damaging and unhelpful piece of news someone could give. They are generalized statistics based on historical data and treatment lines. The oncologist I changed to at my secondary diagnosis in 2020 gave

me the best piece of advise that I still think about....

' Forget what you were told yesterday, each individual is different, and it all depends on how you, as individual, respond to different lines of treatment. Statistics are outdated'

To my greatest achievements in life, George and Henry. I'll never be able to put into words just how much I adore you both and how being your Mum was always written in the stars for me. I will always continue to fight to live for you both as long as entirely possible. I love you both with all my heart. Mum xx

CHAPTER 26

LIZZI ENGLAND

Bump. Meet Lump

I was 29, pregnant, and busy googling whether it was safe to eat brie when the universe decided to play the most twisted game of "Surprise!" ever. Spoiler alert: it wasn't brie that was the problem.

It started with a lump. Not the cute baby bump kind, the kind that makes you stop and go, "Huh. That wasn't there before." This wasn't my fist rodeo and I knew that wasn't normal, even for my balloons of hormonal rebellion. This lump? It was different. Less "miracle of life," more "ominous plot twist."

Being the responsible adult I occasionally pretended to be, I called the doctor. They weren't overly concerned, and for a split second that bought me peace. It was only a few moments later when I was walking out of the room I suddenly thought, this isn't good. A few gropes later, biopsies, and one disturbingly use of the word 'suspicious', I found myself in a cold room waiting for my results.

"It's breast cancer," he said.

And just like that, I was 29, pregnant, and apparently the proud new owner of a malignant tumour.

Now, when you're pregnant, your brain is already on a hormonal rollercoaster. So hearing the words "you have cancer" while also growing a human inside you?

I had questions. So many questions. Was it treatable? What about the baby? What about my other children, they need me!

To my surprise, the medical team was less “doom and gloom” and more “science has come a long way” Apparently, pregnant people can have chemo. Who knew? (Besides all the oncologists, obviously.)

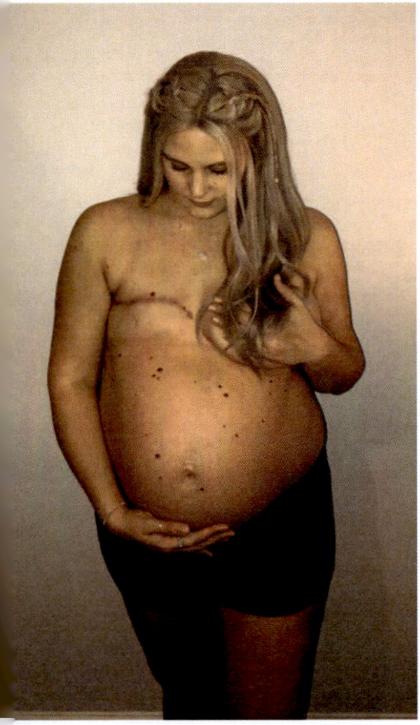

And so began the weirdest baby-moon ever: juggling oncology appointments, crying over baby clothes and not knowing if I should buy any, and also losing my hair. I was growing eyebrows and a baby at the same time, and somehow, one of them was doing better than the other.

There were moments of total absurdity. Like sitting in the chemo chair with a baby doing somersaults in my uterus while I slept, dribbling with an IV in my arm. Or the looks of utter sadness when people would look at me. I felt it too. Somewhere between the cancer and the cravings, something shifted. I realised I wasn’t just fighting for me. I was fighting for that little life growing inside me, who was already more resilient than I could have imagined. (Especially considering they spent their third trimester surrounded by chemo drugs and Celine Dion playlists.)

Let me tell you, nothing will make you feel more like a paradox than people telling you "You're glowing!" when your glow is 90% steroids and nausea.And me? I became a kind of warrior I never wanted to be but damn well learned to respect.

So yes, I got diagnosed with breast cancer at 29 while pregnant. And yes, it sucked. It sucked hard. But it also revealed a version of me that could laugh in waiting rooms, cry in a car park, and still show up for the many ultrasounds with lipstick on and rocking my gorgeous blonde wig!

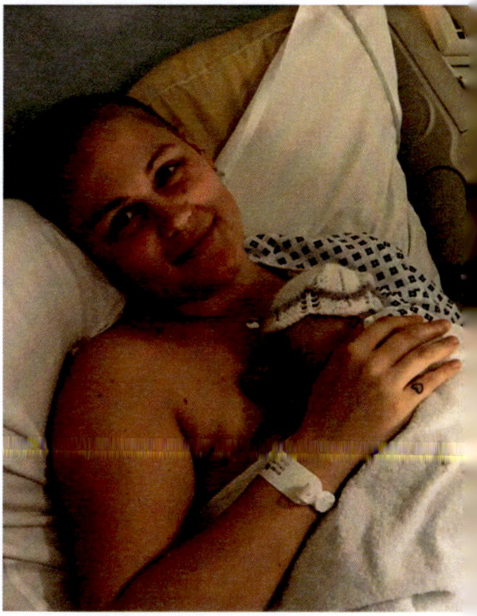

This wasn't the chapter I planned.
But it's the one that made me invincible.
And spoiler alert: both me and the baby?
We made it.

Violet, she arrived strong, healthy and loud. As if to say, "Mum, I got this." And maybe she always did.

I hate that cancer had to crash my pregnancy. But looking back, cancer didn't stand a chance.

Not against me,

Not against Violet,

Not against the two of us, both bald and totally badass.

Plot twist.

The cancer, it came back!

I always wondered if it would come back. Every twinge, every ache, every unusual tiredness made me pause. For seven long months, the doctors failed to take my secondary breast cancer bone pain seriously, dismissing my concerns and attributing the pain to less severe causes without proper investigation. Despite repeatedly describing the intensity and persistence of my symptoms, I was met with vague reassurances and delays in diagnostic testing. I was even told "you're too young for it to be metastatic breast cancer". Bitch please, tell that to the girl who was diagnosed with primary breast cancer at 29 when she was 'too young'.

Their lack of urgency and unwillingness to listen left me feeling invisible and invalidated, while the cancer continued to progress unchecked. This neglect not only delayed critical treatment but also deeply eroded my trust in the healthcare system at a time when I needed support the most.

The words "stage 4", I knew what it meant. I had fought, endured, healed and moved on. Or at least, I thought I had. But cancer doesn't care about timelines or closure. It comes when it wants, and this time, it came back with a vengeance. Stage 4. Metastatic. Words I knew in theory but never expected to own. It was in my bones and boy did I know it.

Grief came in waves. Not just grief for the possibility of dying, but grief for the version of me that thought she was done with this. The woman who celebrated being cancer free. Who dared to imagine life after cancer. I had to mourn her. And them? How would I tell them?

How do you explain to your children that the monster they thought was gone is back and this time, it's not going away?

But here's the thing, even in that grief, something strange happened. I didn't fall apart completely. Maybe because I had already been through the fire once. Or maybe because there's a different kind of strength that shows up when you're staring down the barrel of something you cannot fix. People started saying things like, "You're so brave," or "I don't know how you do it." But I wasn't brave. I was scared, really fucking scared. I didn't "do it" because I was strong—I did it because I had no other choice. You live, or you don't. You fight, or you give up.

This new chapter of my life is not about beating cancer. Stage 4 doesn't work like that. It's about living with cancer. Managing it. Making peace with it. Holding joy and sorrow in the same hand. It's about redefining what hope means not the hope of a cure, but the hope of a full life in whatever time I have.

There are days I still wake up and forget for a few seconds. Then it hits me, like a punch in the gut. But most days, I carry it quietly, like a heavy coat I can't take off, but have learned to wear with grace, no not grace, I lack grace, I wing it. Everyday I get up and I wing it.

The truth is, cancer coming back changed everything. But it didn't take everything. I still laugh. I still love. I still dream. And as long as I'm breathing, I'm still living.
I love you Taylor, Ivy, Teddy & Violet, more than you'll ever know xxxxx

CHAPTER 27

3 YEARS ON - 7 ARE GONE

One Year - Five Ladies Lost

Within just a year of our photoshoot, we faced the devastating loss of Emily, Suzanne, Cathy, Vicky, and Sally. As the anniversaries of their passing come around, I often find myself wondering what they would think of the charity today. I truly believe we would be even more successful if they were still with us because of their commitment, their determination, and their knowledge.

It is often said that when a person dies, a library burns, and this could not be truer of these incredible women. Each one was a source of wisdom, strength, and guidance to so many in their community. Each unique, each with her own story stories that, heartbreakingly, they are no longer here to tell.

Yet, they remain unforgettable. The impression they left on our hearts has never faded; from the moment we first came together in Liverpool. In the months that followed the photoshoot, we achieved so much, and in doing so, our bonds were forged strong, unbreakable, and rooted in the love and courage of those who are no longer with us.

EMILY - HER MUM'S HERO

Died aged 30. Mum to three girls: Isla, Edie, and Anni.
Emily was diagnosed in July 2020 with breast cancer, followed just

three weeks later by a secondary diagnosis in her liver. By June 2021, it had spread to her spine, and by October, to her lymph nodes.

Her mum, Nina, remembers her as devoted to her daughters, with a love for animals, music, and dancing. Emily was kind, selfless, vibrant, and life-loving, with a smile that lit up any room.

Even while enduring chemotherapy, alternative treatments, Covid, and sepsis, Emily never stopped putting her girls first. From her hospital bed, she continued raising funds for secondary breast cancer charities and organising gifts to support others.

On 7th February 2022, Emily passed away with her family by her side, after an undetected spread to her brain caused a fatal haemorrhage. Nina calls Emily "her hero," and her legacy lives on through her daughters and her place within Fighting to be Heard.

SUZANNE - OUR FLOSSY

Died aged 41 Married to John. Devoted daughter of Tommy and Geraldine. Stepmum to Keiran.

Suzanne, known to us all as Flossy, was diagnosed at just 38 with metastatic breast cancer.

She stood proudly with her sisters in the Fighting to be Heard campaign, determined to make a difference. Her commitment inspired her family and friends to raise £1,200 so that we could unite for our official charity launch in March 2022.

Flossy's warmth, determination, and generosity remain woven into the fabric of this charity, and she continues to inspire us in all that we do.

CATHY – GENTLE STRENGTH

Died aged 57 Married to Sean. Mother and stepmother to four. Grandmother to two.

Cathy was diagnosed with secondary breast cancer in February 2021, after discovering a lump in her armpit. The cancer had already metastasized to her liver.

She initially responded well to treatment, with tumours shrinking to the point of becoming almost undetectable. But cancer cells evaded blood marker tests, and by March 2022, scans revealed tumours in her lungs, spine, brain, and liver.

Too unwell for further treatment, Cathy received palliative care, spending her final weeks mostly in hospital due to lung failure.

Cathy embodied gentle strength meeting her illness with grace and determination, while remaining a source of love and steadiness for her family and for us all.

VICKI – OUR ROYAL

Died aged 32 Partner of Gavin. Mum to Grayson and Rey.

Vicki was diagnosed with triple-negative breast cancer in 2018, followed by a secondary diagnosis in 2020. The cancer spread first to her lungs, then to her brain.

To us, she will always be Our Royal. She was a fierce advocate, encouraging others to speak up, fight back, and never settle for less than they deserved. She was constantly researching, seeking treatment options, and generously sharing her knowledge.

Vicki had a heart of gold, a fearless spirit, and an unshakable belief in justice for the secondary breast cancer community.

SALLY – THE SPIRIT OF SAL

Died aged 46. Married to Steve (now Trustee of the charity). Mum to James and Joe.

Sally was diagnosed with triple-negative breast cancer in 2019. Despite surgery, chemotherapy, and radiotherapy, the cancer returned just 18 months later. It spread to her kidneys, causing serious complications.

The last time many of us saw Sal was after a lovely evening at her home. We dropped her at the hospital, not knowing it would be the final goodbye. She never came home again.

Sally's greatest wish was to fight for change, to support the underdog, and to create a better future for those who came after. The Fighting to be Heard Foundation was built on the Spirit of Sal and her legacy continues to guide every step we take.

2022 - Losing 25% of our ladies' women who were never just

statistics, the brutal facts of this disease were unravelling before our eyes. Losing Emily, Suzanne, Cathy, Vicki, and Sally left a void that could never be filled, yet their light, courage, and determination continue to guide us.

In collaboration with their families, we agreed that the image needed to change, it had to provoke greater awareness and reflect the stark reality of what the secondary breast cancer community faced.

Sane Seven re-edited the original image, creating a profoundly shocking portrayal that became a catalyst for conversation and awareness during Breast Cancer Awareness Month in 2023.

One minute, our models were looking fabulous and glamorous in a photoshoot. From the outside, you would never know they were living with an incurable diagnosis. On the surface, people assumed they couldn't possibly be dying and, if I am honest, I thought the same that day. How ignorant I was.

I learnt quickly that the reality was very different to the brave faces these ladies put on day in and day out. Within just one year, five of those new friends were gone.

2023 - No more heartbreak this year, we had endured more than our share in the first year of our friendship. It felt as though our photoshoot family was defying the odds, standing strong together against a disease that had already taken too much. Treatments were holding the bastard at bay, and for a while, we allowed ourselves to hope that time might just be on their side.

2024 - we had launched the charity. Alongside Kate Rackham and Gill Corry, I found not only partners but true friends. Through our shared experiences of building a start-up charity, we came to know each other's strengths and weaknesses, and it was never a one-way street. It wasn't just me caring about their health and families, they gave me back more than I could have ever imagined. They were the best friends I could wish for, and they carried me through so much too.

I often forgot they had cancer, because, as we say in Liverpool, they were hard as nails. Our relationships across the charity grew stronger by the day: Nikki Williams and I became firm besties; Lisa Jones, our Welsh lass, calls me Pasty after I once asked, in a menopause moment, if anyone else smelt like a pasty from time to time. The nickname stuck. So many funny but sad times bonded us together.

GILL CORY

Gill began to suffer and had a few stays in hospital. I cherish the lunches we shared in between, seeing our Joan Collins in her element at her Fashion Show by her favourite Coco Boutique. The time we sat together at Marina Dalglish's Centre in Aintree Hospital. Will forever be an example of Gills strength. Gill, hooked up to IV Chemo, wearing her cold cap always determined to save her hair and beauty and yet there we were, running a finance meeting about the Winter Grants as we had a deadline. A man and woman sitting beside us asked what we were working on, and Gill, with such pride, announced that she was the treasurer of our charity. They celebrated her achievements, and she beamed with pride.

Gill had always been a proud woman she was the youngest female magistrate in Sefton. Even through her illness, she powered on with dignity and commitment when her hope was waning, she didn't stop the fight to help others. Nikki and I visited her in the hospice to say our goodbyes, and it wasn't long before she left us.

When I was asked to speak at her service, it was a privilege I will never forget. Four of our charity family attended that day: Nikki, Laura Shutt, Kate Enell, and me. The reality of being at Gill's funeral was almost too much to bear, Kate had to leave, overcome with grief.

Yet even in loss, Gill's spirit remains a part of our foundation. Her pride, her dignity, and her determination to keep giving back even while wired up to chemo live on in the work we do today.

KATE RACKHAM

It's 3:30 a.m. and I can't sleep. This feels like the right time to write about Kate no interruptions, just space to think about what this formidable woman brought to our charity and the legacy she left behind.

First of all, she was funny. Sarcastic too, just like Gill. The two of them would leave me standing while they ripped into me good job I loved them, because they never held back. I did get my revenge one day, though. I told Kate I'd meet her at the Quarter Café in town, and she ended up going to the one on Mathew Street. Surrounded by a hen party of cowgirls, she was not amused. Let's just say "Dickhead" was among her choice words for me that day. She was fond of calling me that, and we laughed about it for ages.

And then there were her tweets. Not just the one that went viral and sent her message around the globe, but the ones she was so proud of, the ones that got a few hundred likes. She'd phone me in delight, saying, "This Twitter's where we need to focus. Sod the rest, I'm not into that Insta. My tweet's gone viral!" I'd smile and agree, because you didn't want to disagree with Kate. Maybe it was something in the name Kate's, both with a bit of kick-off in us.

When I say my heart broke the day I went to say goodbye to my mate, I mean it. Hearing her wishes for the charity I hold so dear to my heart, and which now run through the pages of this book and the veins of our charity. This was one of the hardest moments of my life seeing my beautiful friend for the last time.

Kate and I had danced together, laughed together, and yes, even drunk pints together. She took me right back to my student days in Manchester with her, the vibe was always cool, and the tunes always mint. Her rendition of Mr Wendle on the dance floor word for word, with her groove perfectly captured on video is something I still look back on whenever I need to see her gorgeous face.

She loved music, especially The Blossoms. She took her girls to see them for their very first concert, and she never stopped playing their tracks. The number of times I reached out to their team, hoping to get them to perform at one of our events, was ridiculous. So, if anyone reading this knows The Blossoms get in touch with Mark at Barking Dog, Urmston! She would fume with me I didn't use this book to get that gig sorted.

But here I am, circling and avoiding what is hardest to write: how

Kate's loss has impacted me personally, and our charity. It's almost too painful to put into words. I miss her check-ins, our planning WhatsApp blowing up whenever she had an idea. Every single day, Kate poured herself into her family, her teaching, and this charity. We miss her gumption and her doing nature she didn't procrastinate she did. Just like did every day her minutes were used wisely. She would hare with me her diary for the week, and it was jam packed with meet ups and her life was full to the brim. Our world was robbed of her goodness

The girl with the biggest smile stole all our hearts. Her loss left a void so deep it has taken the charity time to recover from such a colossal absence.

Mark and I were called upon to speak about her passing on BBC News. We sat together for half an hour beforehand, crying into our coffees, unable to believe we were there without her. People later said we held it together well, but they hadn't seen us in those moments leading up to it. We put on our brave faces for the girl who had turned that act into a fine art.

She was a natural public speaker. We rolled her out for every occasion because she could hold a room like no one else. Honestly, she could have been a presenter, she had that gift with people. She had the X factor in every way. Her voice wasn't just prolific in the secondary breast cancer community here in the UK it carried globally thanks to UK activity on X.

I am certain she is smiling down now at the impact she made. At that point, I truly didn't think we could take any more.

I didn't sign up for this on the 26th of September 2021. And yet, here I am.

It was like the best relationship you can imagine, a whirlwind romance, meeting your soulmate as junior school, someone who gets you, laughs at the same things, and changes your life for the better. Then boom they are gone.

I own my grief, and I own the guilt of feeling so sad. I carry it in her memory. It's all her fault, really for being so good.

I am obviously not just grieving for myself. I grieve for the loved ones missing their mums, wives, sisters, and daughters for the families now raising children without them, for the grandparents stepping in to raise their grandchildren. So, we carry on for Kate and the promises made.

KATIE ENELL

When we thought things couldn't get any worse, November 11th, 2024, Remembrance Day brought the worst year on record to its penultimate point. It was the year of unlimited grief.

She was our Kate. Our baby Kate. My friend. Nikki's "charity daughter." The one we all protected.

In the words of a favourite song that will always remind us of Kate: "People come into our lives for a reason." And she certainly did.

I had known her for a while locally, through social media. When I heard she had secondaries, I introduced her to Gill Cory for support. Gill felt the same protective instinct over her, just as I did. We all did. She left a handprint on our hearts, and we were all changed for the better.

Kate had called me from Aintree Hospital. She hadn't wanted to tell anyone she was in because her mum and dad were on holiday. She had just had great scan results, sharing on 26th October on Instagram her scan was stable, her cancer hasn't spread or grown for 6 months and #livelifetothefullest So she'd begged her parents to go, telling them it was the best time to take a break. She didn't want anyone to worry her mum and da so I kept it to myself for a few days.

She then told Nikki later that she was fine she'd just had a sausage roll, Liam was with her, there was no need for us to go in. She sounded okay. But at 7 p.m., Nikki phoned to say we needed to get to the hospital. Kate had taken a turn for the worse.

We arrived at Aintree, and our hearts broke. I can't share more, out of respect for her family and the heartbreak her mum and dad have lived through. But her life turned on a sixpence that day, and it showed us again just how fragile life is. One minute you're getting a stable scan and feeling the relief of hope and just a few weeks later, we had to say goodbye.

It was only one month earlier, on the 4th of October, that Katie, Nikki, and I joined Roy Basnett's Feel Good Friday show on Liverpool Live Radio station, thanks to an invite from positivity psychologist Liz Folan. Katie loved being on the show. Her bravery shone through she didn't appear to be near the end at all. She was full of life, vibrant, and determined.

At the time, Katie was sharing "a day in the life" posts every single day throughout Octobers Breast Cancer Awareness Month. Just five weeks and three days later, we lost her. That day changed me for good.

Another funeral. Another remembrance speech. Another packed service, filled with family, friends, and her charity family all broken.

Losing Kate that night will never leave me or Nikki. Remembrance Day remembers those who fought for the sake of us all, and in so many ways, it was a fitting day to lose our baby Kate. But her passing also finished us. Gill, Kate, and now Katie. We were done.

Our charity fell silent.

CHAPTER 28

THE FINAL TWEET

1.82 BILLION VIEWS ACROSS THE WORLD
UK – USA – IRELAND – GERMANY – TURKEY – UAE – VIETNAM – EGYPT - CHEQ REPUBLIC – NEW ZEALAND - CANADA

On 14 June 2024, the world read the words Kate Rackham @ teacherwithcancer had prepared:

"If you're reading this, it means I have died. But do not cry for me. I have lived my life on my own terms, the way I have wanted to. I joined X because I needed an outlet, what I got was so much more. You made me feel validated in my feelings and much less alone. Thank you."

Her words were left with her husband Mark and sister Caroline to post on X (formerly Twitter) after her death a final act of courage and clarity. What began as a deeply personal farewell quickly became a global headline, sparking conversation and compassion across continents.

UK Media Response
The impact of her final message was felt first in Britain.

· ITV News Granada broke the story with: "If you're reading this, I have died: Manchester breast cancer activist's final message".

· BBC North West Tonight followed with emotional interviews.

Kate's husband, Mark, spoke of his loss, his pride, and the depth of her legacy, and I shared how her charity would carry her fight on and how her tenacity had laid the foundations of the charity even during her last and difficult months.

· National titles such as The Independent, Evening Standard, The Sun, The Mirror, and broadcasters including LBC amplified the story.

· Regional outlets, including the Lancaster Guardian, shared the story across their networks, ensuring Kate's words reached homes across the UK.

The Story Goes Global - The reach began to multiply reaching extraordinary figures.

According to the Meltwater report, Kates final tweet on her account has been viewed 41 million times, and the media reach is 1.82 billion to date.

Kate's "final tweet" to her 17,000 X followers did not remain confined to the UK, it travelled the world:

· The Independent (international edition) amplified her words for global audiences.

· Yahoo News and AOL syndicated her story widely across the US.

· In Australia, news.com.au ran: "Teacher, 39, announces own death after dying from cancer."

· In Germany, FOCUS Online published: “Mutter verkündet eigenen Krebs-Tod via Twitter – was Brustkrebs so tückisch macht.”

· In Spain, La Vanguardia carried her message under the headline: “No lloréis por mí…”.

· Across the U.S. Hispanic and Latin American world, Telemundo / Hoy Día shared: “Si estás leyendo esto, significa que he muerto”, noting her post had been viewed more than 40 million times.

Lord Jim Knight, who sits in the House of Lords, paid tribute to Ms Rackham, saying: “This made me stop today and turn off the noise. Such dignity.”

Legacy in the Digital Age

Kate’s scheduled tweet shows the extraordinary power of a single message in the digital age. In life, she was a teacher, campaigner, Co founder and friend; in death, her words became a beacon of dignity and defiance, sparking headlines in multiple languages.

It also showed the power of our social channels for the good. In the days that followed, people all over the world searched for information on secondary breast cancer. Our website saw record views, proof that her voice turned grief into awareness.

With that global attention comes responsibility and opportunity.

Most of all, Kate’s words were not written as a rallying cry, but as a thank you.

A conversation with her audience, her X community, her family of supporters whom she held so dear. Her final post was her way of saying: "I see you, I am grateful for you, and please don't cry for me."

Kate's "Final Tweet" was not just a goodbye it was an act of love. A message that continues to connect her with the rest of the world, reminding us that even in her absence, her voice carries on the conversations she began.

In 2024, 1.8 billion reached. 2025, a further 281 million reach.

It is without doubt Kate Rackham raised Global awareness of Secondary, Stage 4 , Metastatic Incurable Breast Cancer.

She is smiling down.

CHAPTER 29

HOW FAR WE HAVE COME

When we began this journey, none of us could have imagined the scale of what would be possible. What started with a shared determination to be heard has grown into something far greater a lifeline for women navigating the challenges of secondary breast cancer.

Grants may look like numbers on a page, but behind every figure is a story, a moment of relief, a spark of joy, or a little less weight on someone's shoulders. Our community has shown that small acts of support, repeated and shared, create a powerful ripple effect. Year after year, our grants have been a tangible expression of care.

Seasonal Grants

Summer 2023 28 recipients £9,800 awarded

Our first summer grants marked a milestone. Each award was not just financial support but recognition of the women at the heart of this movement.

Winter 2023 50 recipients £25,000 awarded

As winter came, we doubled our reach. The need was greater, and so was our resolve. £25,000 brought comfort during a season often filled with extra challenges.

Summer 2024 83 recipients £33,200 awarded

Momentum was building. More women applied, more stories poured in, and with them came proof that our mission mattered. Over £33,000 was shared, offering vital breathing space to those who needed it most.

Winter 2024 114 recipients £31,920 awarded

The figures told their own story: we were growing stronger. To support more than a hundred women in one season was a testament to what community and determination can achieve together.

Summer 2025 133 recipients £26,600 awarded

This summer was our most impactful yet 133 grants given, 133 lives touched. Each grant may not solve everything, but it creates a moment of dignity and relief, a chance to exhale.

The Total So Far

408 grants in total £126,520 paid out to date

And the story does not end there. Alongside our seasonal grants, we have also given discretionary grants to families facing extreme financial hardship. These moments cannot always wait for the next funding cycle sometimes, help is needed immediately. By stepping in, we have eased burdens such as urgent household bills, travel costs to hospital appointments, or the simple necessities that so many take for granted.

Survey Feedback

To ensure our support truly meets the needs of our community, we asked recipients to share their experiences. The responses were clear and compelling:

Has your diagnosis impacted you financially?

Yes – 98%

Almost every person we support has faced significant financial consequences alongside their diagnosis.

How did you use your grant?

Rent/Mortgage – 8.9%
Utility bills – 61.1%
Food – 24.7%

The majority of grants went toward life's most basic essentials. They are not luxuries—they are about keeping the heating on, the lights working, and food on the table.

Are you aware of any other charities that provide financial support to Secondary Breast Cancer patients?

Yes – 22 (11.6%)
No – 168 (88.4%)

This striking result highlights the unique and vital role of Fighting to be Heard. For most, we are the only place they know to turn for financial support at such a critical time.

Voices from Our Community

Behind every grant is a life changed, a burden lifted, or a memory made possible. Our community's words speak more powerfully than any statistic:

"I have been very fortunate to receive help from Fighting to be Heard. My cancer diagnosis has meant life has become a real struggle financially. The grants have enabled me to put the heating on so my elderly parents could stay at Christmas. Without it, we would have spent it apart. To be able to keep my home warm during the winter months and spend time with my parents (who live 200 miles away) was so special and meaningful. I can never thank you enough for giving us this time together. You are all bloody marvellous and while I wish there was not a need for you, I am so, so grateful that you are here. Thank you from my family and me."

"Thank you so much, this has helped me to bring up my baby and child whilst going through this terrible time."

"The support I have received from Fighting to be Heard has been overwhelming. I have been able to make some very special memories with my children and family. I can no longer work so financially it has also helped. To have this support means more than I can put into words."

"As a group, the ladies of Fighting to be Heard are approachable, fierce and passionate and I feel an affiliation with you all. I admire your tenacity and hard work and am so, so appreciative of the work you do. Receiving grants helped massively with a large bill that hits at Christmas time and allowed me to afford time with family in the summer. I'm forever grateful."

"Words are inadequate in the way your financial help impacted me. I was so worried about the cost of energy I felt unable to keep myself warm it was miserable. You gave me back that freedom. I will never forget and remain forever grateful."

"I just really want to say thank you. I have had to stop working due to my diagnosis and to lose a whole salary in a household is such a big hit, especially as I was the main earner. I'm so glad to still be here five years on, but living five years with no income is tough. I got cancer in and around my pregnancy with my only child and the pressure to make memories is real. Thank you for helping that to happen and also contributing to paying out winter fuel which isn't something I ever thought I'd have to worry about. However, when you're home 90% of the time it is horrendous. I now completely empathise with the elderly heating themselves and not a whole house. I never thought I'd have to live like this, but we are where we are. Thank you, thank you, thank you."

"The financial grant support is invaluable. I don't have the words to say how grateful I am for the support I have received. I have been able to make memories with my family. I cannot thank you enough. The work you do to support patients like me is just amazing. Thank you."

This is how far we have come: not only in the funds we have distributed, but in the lives we have touched. Every figure is matched by a story, every grant by a voice. Together, they tell a single truth: Fighting to be Heard is more than a charity it is a community, a safety net, and a promise that no one faces this journey alone.

OUR FIRST AGM

On 29th September 2024, we held our very first Annual General Meeting. It was a moment of reflection and planning, a chance to review all that we had achieved together and to look towards to the future. We gathered in our happy place the Lakeside at Crosby, along the beach where the calm surroundings provided the perfect setting for such an important day.

People dialled in from across the UK, joining their voices to ours. We broke into groups to share ideas and shape our thoughts for the year ahead, ensuring that everyone had a voice in guiding the direction of the charity.

It was also a day of mixed emotions. With the passing of Gill Cory and Kate Rackham, their absence was deeply felt. Yet the presence of Kate Enell, who attended despite struggling with her health, lifted us all. Her brilliance shone through, sparking ideas that have since been carried out in the work we do today. Mark Rackham, Kate's husband attended, this was so challenging for him but still he came and sat beside us for Kate.

Our first AGM was more than a meeting; it was a marker of how far we had come and a promise of what was still to come. We now look forward to our next AGM in November, following the launch of our book and the This Is Me event.

FIGHTING
TO BE HEARD

FIGHTING
TO BE HEARD
We can't fight for our lives.
We are incurable.
We are fighting to be heard.
Fighting for a voice for the 61,000 patients living with secondary breast cancer in the UK.
FIGHTING
TO BE HEARD

AWARDS

Winning Merseyside Inspirational Woman of the Year 2024 at the MWOTY Awards was an honour I will never forget, though the day was bittersweet. I was deep in grief after burying Kate Rackham on Monday, and only six weeks earlier, Gill Cory. If truth be told, I didn't feel like going at all. My mum reassured me with her gentle way "it will be okay, love," and my Auntie Lib asked what award I was up for. I honestly didn't know much about MWOTY before the nomination. Yet, walking into that room filled with amazing women the "Quietly Brilliant," as Ellie Kerr so beautifully puts it, something shifted.

Everyone at my table meant the world to me: my family, my charity sisters, Nikki, Kate, and Kim. We were broken, but together, holding each other up. When my name was announced, my girls stood beside me, rightly so, because this award was never about me alone it was about our charity's achievements, all of us, symbiotic, one with the other. Behind the smiles, there was deep heartache, but I spoke about it openly in my speech, with my girls next to me. I dedicated the award to Gill and Kate. Now that my Kate Enell has gone, who looked stunning in her pink dress, the day has taken on an even greater importance; it's a precious memory that I hold close to my heart. I am forever grateful to my dear friend Hilda Yarker for nominating me, and to the Queen of MWOTY, Ellie Kerr, for giving our charity a platform and a gift we will always treasure. Thank you for the ride, Ellie, and for the opportunities, the friendships, and introducing me to your network of women who lift each other up. My charity family are, and always will be, the most inspirational women I have ever known.

ersey
WONGS

planning

Merseyside
WOMEN
YEAR

Butterfly Awards 2024, I was personally nominated by Sharon Tickle, a friend of Seema Malhotra, who I had the privilege of being introduced to. It was a beautiful evening, guided so warmly by the lovely Sarah Pickle, the orchestrator of the awards. I was honoured to be a finalist and shared the night with Nikki, my mum, and Rachel – the daughter of our much-loved Gill Cory. Together, we celebrated Gill's life through her daughter's presence, which made the evening especially poignant.

2025, we returned again as finalists in the Charity Impact Award. This time, it was my privilege to nominate the incredible women from our charity who, despite living with an incurable diagnosis themselves, work tirelessly to support others in the very same community. To no one's surprise, they won. Seeing Lisa Jones, Laura Shutt, and Nikki Williams recognised all trustees and true inspirations was a moment of immense pride. Sean Snape and Nikki Williams collected the award on behalf of the charity, and we celebrated together, knowing the recognition was so deeply deserved.

Winner
CHARITY IMPACT TEAM AWARD
Butterfly Breast Cancer Awards

CHARITY IMPACT TEAM AWARD
MAKE 2NDS COUNT
BREAST FRIENDS
Make 2NDS Count
Breast Friends
SPONSORED BY DC LOMAS

VOLUNTARY LED

Our foundation is entirely community-led, founded and delivered by individuals affected by secondary breast cancer. Every aspect of what we do is shaped by lived experience whether through a personal diagnosis or as someone closely impacted by it. This gives our work authenticity, empathy, and strength that cannot be manufactured.

We are proud that Fighting to be Heard is powered by volunteers and trustees who dedicate their time, energy, and voices to supporting others. Their contributions ensure that our grants, campaigns, and community support remain grounded in real life, real needs, and real impact.

We would like to extend our heartfelt thanks to all of our volunteers: Ava May Tobin, Rachel Faye, Rosalie Galvin, Charlotte Rose, Marilyn Kinch, Christine Orr, Elizabeth Chapman, Phil Aldo, Chris Jones, Kate Jones, and Sophie Chapman.

Your commitment makes our mission possible.

OUR CHARITY FAMILY

Honouring the Courage and Commitment of Our Volunteers and Trustees Living with Secondary Breast Cancer.

At the heart of our charity lies an extraordinary group of women each living with the life-limiting diagnosis of Secondary Breast Cancer (SBC) who selflessly dedicate their time, energy, and compassion to support others across the UK navigating the same devastating journey.

These remarkable women are not only fighting their own battles but continue to reach outward, offering strength, understanding, and practical help to patients and families affected by SBC. Despite the daily physical and emotional toll of their condition, they volunteer tirelessly to ensure no one feels alone.

Laura Shutt, our dedicated Secretary, embodies resilience and service. Formerly a teacher, Laura had to leave her beloved profession due to her diagnosis. Yet, she channels her energy into leading our grant-giving programme and supporting administrative functions with quiet determination and professionalism. Her contributions are even more inspiring when one considers that she is also the devoted mother of young Charlotte, who has just started school. Laura's ability to balance motherhood, her illness, and her volunteering role is nothing short of exceptional.

"I became a trustee because I truly believe in everything Fighting to be Heard stands for. I'm fortunate to have an incredible support network of family and friends who not only help me live a fulfilling life but also inspire me to use my voice to create change for future generations. No family should ever feel alone or isolated because of their condition and that's why this charity means so much to me." Laura Shutt

Lisa Jones, Patient, Trustee, Head of Support Group & TikTok (March 2nd 2023 – to date) a loving mother of three daughters, gives her time to support our closed online group a vital lifeline where SBC patients and family members find solace, connection, and a space to speak freely. Lisa also plays a key role in our social media presence and fundraising activities, helping to raise both awareness and essential funds. Her warm presence and deep empathy have created a safe and supportive environment for many.

"Being a part of this amazing charity fills me with warmth. I knew the day I was diagnosed I wanted to navigate my sadness into helping others. Supporting others fills my cup. And I couldn't be surrounded by better people to work alongside in doing so. It's been an honour and privilege to be a part of something so amazing. What a legacy! Mae o wedi bod yn braint fod yn rhan o rhywbeth mor wych! Am cymynrodd!" Lisa Jones

Nikki Williams, Patient, Trustee, Head of Outreach (March 2nd 2023 – to date) a retired nurse and fellow patient, leads our outreach programme with immense compassion and sensitivity. With her clinical background and lived experience, Nikki has an extraordinary ability to connect with others. She regularly visits patients in their homes to offer comfort, guidance, and a listening ear. Her approach is gentle, human, and deeply appreciated by those she helps. She also supports our wider fundraising initiatives, always willing to go the extra mile for the cause.

"As a trustee it has been overwhelming to see the responses we have had from those receiving the grants. Something that was a pipe dream three years ago at Sally's funeral has come to life and is now a much-needed commodity and a lifeline for secondary breast cancer patients and their families. Being a trustee has given me a new purpose – to reach out and help others in a similar situation." Nikki Williams

Each of these women gives something so precious, their time, something they know the true value of. Their courage, kindness, and commitment exemplify the very best of humanity.

Our charity stands today because of the strength, determination, and vision of those who have given their hearts and precious time to its foundation. Among them, three extraordinary women Kate Rackham, Gill Cory, and Kate Enell played vital roles as Cofounders and Trustees. Their dedication, love, and commitment to the cause helped shape Fighting to be Heard into the lifeline it is today.

They gave selflessly, often when their own strength was most tested, to ensure that women with Secondary Breast Cancer had a voice, a community, and the support they so deeply deserved. Their legacy is woven into every grant given, every family supported, and every patient who finds comfort in our work.

We honour them here, not only as Trustees but as cherished friends and inspiring women whose impact will never be forgotten.

TRUSTEES' VOICES

The strength of Fighting to be Heard lies not only in the women at its heart but also in those who stand alongside them, ensuring the charity has the guidance, stability, and vision it needs to thrive. Our Trustees carry both professional expertise and deeply personal reasons for their involvement. Their voices reflect the shared commitment that drives our mission forward.

Lou Chadwick – Finance Lead (March 2nd, 2023 – until the passing of her best friend, Co-Founder & Secretary, Kate Rackham)

Best Friend of Co-Founder & Secretary, Kate Rackham
"Becoming a trustee was my way of supporting my best friend, Kate, as she helped build a lifeline for women with secondary breast cancer. The charity gave her purpose and strength, and today it carries her legacy forward. For me, it will always be a tribute to her courage, her vision, and our friendship."

Rob Shutt – Finance Lead, Trustee (2023 – to date) Husband of Laura Shutt (Patient, Trustee & Secretary, 2023–to date)

"My amazing wife's journey with secondary breast cancer makes Fighting To Be Heard deeply personal to me. The work that the charity does gives strength, friendship and a voice to those impacted by the incurable disease, and I am honoured to be able to support the charity alongside my wife and others as a Trustee."

Sean Snape – Trustee (March 2nd 2023 – to date) Husband of Cathy Snape (Founder) "From the outset of meeting these amazing and selfless women on that fateful day in Liverpool, I have been in awe of the tireless work and dedication they show to the Fighting to Be Heard movement.

From first-hand experience I have witnessed the good that they do – the fundraising, the mentoring, the peer-to-peer support for each other and for those who are lost and alone. They reach out to help people make sense of what they are facing. A sisterhood of support exists here, one that shares knowledge and experiences both positive and painful to help steer and guide you through the minefield that a secondary breast cancer diagnosis throws you into.

So much love and support is given and received within this organisation of volunteers that it is truly heart-warming to see and to be a small part of. I am very proud of this wonderful and talented group of people I am lucky enough to call my friends."

Steve Nyland – Trustee (March 2nd 2023 – to date) Husband of Sally Nyland (Founder) "As Sally's husband I was approached to be a trustee, where I am able to keep Sally's voice alive. Sometimes I feel she is tapping me on the shoulder and pointing me in the right direction."

Mark Rackham – Volunteer (March 2nd 2023 – to date)
"I'm very proud of Fighting to Be Heard and what it has achieved to support patients and their families. It is great for me and my children to see the legacy of Kate live on through the charity's work. I know from 1st hand experience the huge difference the charity makes to people living with this awful disease, and I will continue to support the charity in any way that I am able."

Charlotte Ashton – Volunteer (March 2nd 2023 – to date)

“My name is Charlotte and I am a volunteer for fighting to be heard because of my mum Nikki, who is the founder and a patient of the charity. I volunteer so I can support her and stand by her. I volunteer to help fight to be heard for everyone.”

Having it made me stronger, that's for sure,
A journey of resilience, a battle to endure.
Through the darkest nights, I found inner light,
A spirit unwavering, shining ever so bright.

In the face of adversity, I stood tall,
Fighting with every ounce of strength, giving it my all.
It tried to break me, but I refused to fall,
A warrior emerged, standing proud and standing tall.

Through the pain and tears, I discovered my might,
A newfound courage, like a beacon in the night.
I faced my fears head on, embraced the unknown,
Finding strength within myself that had previously been unknown.

It taught me lessons, profound and deep,
To cherish every moment, to treasure and keep.
It showed me the power of love and support,
From family and friends, a lifeline of comfort.

So though the journey was tough, I emerged with grace,
A survivor, a fighter, with a smile on my face.
It made me stronger, it tested my core,
But I rose above it all, and I'll keep fighting forevermore.

Ava May Tobin – Markting (March 2nd 2023 – to date)

"The first time I heard the words secondary breast cancer was when my mum's friend, Kate, was diagnosed and, heartbreakingly, later passed away.

My own journey with Fighting to Be Heard began soon after, during a campaign photoshoot at Liverpool Boxing Gym. I was eighteen, about to start university, and working in a salon as a makeup artist with a knack for organisation. My mum asked if I could help with the photoshoot, coordinating the day and doing makeup for some of the women. Of course, I said yes.

Up until then, I'd been pretty naïve about the different types of cancer. The only close encounter I had was when my best friend had leukaemia when we were in high school, thankfully, now she's been in remission for four years. But breast cancer was just breast cancer to me, I didn't know anything about secondaries. Not one thing.

On 26 September 2021, I stepped into the gym and met a room full of women who, to me, didn't look ill at all. They certainly didn't look like they were living with incurable secondary cancer. They looked, as people might say, "normal." That day changed my entire perspective on life.

My first makeup client was Sally, My Sal, and from that moment, the rest is history. Words can hardly capture who she was: kind, caring, an angel on earth. Our bond grew quickly and deeply that day and remained strong until the heartbreaking moment we lost her.

Sal's words always calmed me, she was patient, and her hugs could make anything better. What I'd give for one of those hugs now as I write this.

Sal was determined and full of spirit. On the day of her funeral, the charity truly came to life.

My mum

Where do I even begin about her? I wouldn't even be involved with this charity if it wasn't for her. By now you've heard her name, Kate, my greatest inspiration.

It's 2:00 a.m. on September 29, 2025, and she's sitting right beside me, just as she has every night for the past two weeks. While we write and edit this book, whilst she's simultaneously planning our "This Is Me" show and keeping up with her full-time job and home life. That alone speaks for itself. Selfless.

You've also heard about The Power of Three - Kate, Gill and Mum. That name isn't just for show. The three of them truly thrived together. Three determined Northerners whose energy filled the charity with so much love and compassion.

But unfortunately, we lost Gill, and then Kate not long after, it shook us all. For my mum, it was devastating. The sparkle in her light dimmed, and for a while it felt as though part of her was missing.

Yet even through the darkness, she kept showing up. For our family and for the charity, even though it was so hard for her without her two sidekicks. Her commitment to honouring her friends' memories is what keeps the charity alive.

My mum has been at the heart of it all, volunteering countless hours to coordinate events, manage outreach, and make sure every story is heard. She's the kind of person who will spend her evenings and weekends helping with fundraising plans, comforting families, or simply listening when someone needs to talk.

As her daughter, I see the behind-the-scenes version of Kate. Does the laptop ever close? Hardly. She's the most hardworking, dedicated person I've ever met, and anyone who knows her would say the same.

Mum pours her heart into making sure no story goes unheard. Her passion helps the foundation raise awareness, fund grants, and give patients the platform they deserve.

Her commitment to this cause and to everyone around her is precisely why I'm proud to stand beside her and keep the charity alive. Creating this book and using my skills has been an honour. I hope Sal, Gill, Kate and baby Kate are all proud of what we have all achieved."

DEFINITELY

EVENTS TO DATE

Some of the events we have supported, and others created by incredible individuals, continue to inspire us with their commitment, creativity, and community spirit. Each one has played a vital role in raising funds, awareness, and togetherness. We are deeply grateful to everyone who has poured their time, energy, and hearts into making these moments possible.

2023

· Moel Famau Walk – June 2023, organised by Lisa Jones (Founder & Trustee).

· Em Fest – October 2023, organised by Nina Cooper, mum of Emily (founder).

· Masquerade Charity Ball – 25th October 2023, Chester, organised by Kimberley (founder) & Sean Noble.

· Fizzy Friday in Memory of Sally – organised by Steve Nyland (trustee) and friends, honouring Sally Nyland (founder).

· Glam It Up Wear It Pink Event – September 2023, in memory of Sarah Cheers, organised by Ann Cheers and family.

· Wizards & Witches Halloween Party – October 2023, in memory of Emily (founder), organised by Nina, family & friends.

· Coco Fashion Show – November 2023, organised by Nicola Johnson and Gill Cory (co-founder & treasurer).

· Floristry Day in Memory of Sarah Cheers – 6th November 2023, organised by Auntie Dianne.

· Real Housewives Charity Launch – with thanks to CRLab UK sponsors and celebrities.

2024

· Listen Up – 1st Event – 13th January 2024, organised by Kate Rackham (co-founder & secretary) and husband Mark Rackham.

· Trinity Logistics Event – 1st March 2024, organised by Amanda Unsworth, Trinity Logistics.

· MMA Charity Match – 13th May 2024, in memory of Sally Nyland, organised by Tom Redfern and James Nyland, match-funded by Toyota.

· Sparta Derby FC Charity Match – July 2024, organised by Joe & James, sons of Sally and Steve, in memory of Sally Nyland (founder).

· Deralam Celebrity Golf Day – 22nd July 2024, organised by Steve McMahon.

Golfers included: Tony Bellew (Boxer), Stan Boardman (Comedian), Rudimental (DJ), Jim Beglin, Phil Thompson, and Ronnie Whelan (Footballers).

Sponsors included: Paramount Digital, Panorama Kitchens, Clay Bank Estates, Topform, Barons Furniture.

Halloween Welly Walk – 20th October 2024, Sefton Park Liverpool, organised by Laura Shutt (trustee & secretary).

· Community Social in Mold – 27th October 2024, organised by Lisa Jones (trustee & founder).

· Brew Chimps Birthday Party for Kate Rackham – November 2024, organised by Tracey & David, with thanks to all who joined.

· New Year's Party – 31st December 2024, Cartref Caravan Camping Park, in memory of Emily Roberts.

2025

· Classic Memories – 13th May 2025, at Barking Dog Urmston, organised by Mark Rackham.

· Tattoo Event at Deva Vitrix Chester – 20th July 2025, in memory of Sarah Cheers, with thanks to Ami Harris, Rachel & Sarah.

· Listen Up – 2nd Event – 25th January 2025, Manchester, organised by Mark Rackham & friends.

Special Mentions

· St Joseph's Catholic Primary School – for hosting a number of charity fundraisers in honour of Kate Rackham's school where she taught.

· Sainsbury's Crosby – for permitting a bag-packing fundraiser, organised by our dedicated volunteer Rachel Faye.

DJ QUOTES - LISTEN UP

Dave Haslam: "I always loved seeing Kate on the dancefloor and out and about; she had such spirit, it sparkled the first time I met her just after the millennium and if anything, that energy and positivity grew as she got older, and, unbelievably, when she got ill. An inspirational young woman."

Clint Boon: ""I'll never forget Kate. One of the most inspiring human beings I've ever met. She had the most beautiful smile and a wonderful spirit. I feel blessed to have known her."

Justine Alderman (Across The Tracks): "All my best memories with Kate are at gigs, festivals or clubs - this is the best way I can think of to celebrate her life and legacy."

Martin Glynn (Across The Tracks): "Kate was such a force of nature, she truly understood the value of life. Her teaching didn't just stop at school. Her greatest lesson was to show us, by example, how important it is to make the most of it... to celebrate and cherish what you've got and whenever you can, try to make a positive difference."

Huw Thomas (DJ Adverse Camber): "A sense of mischief and smile that would illuminate every room she entered."

Matt Robey: ""I was djing in Lancaster last March, and Kate came down to the night, which I didn't expect. On the dancefloor, I asked what she was drinking, and she said 'lemonade, I'm driving back to Manchester tonight because I have Chemo in the morning'. I just thought that was amazing and said so much about her character. She stayed until 1am."

OUR FUNDRAISING HEROES

From the very beginning, our community has stepped forward with courage, creativity, and determination. Each of you has gone above and beyond pushing your own personal boundaries, taking on challenges big and small, and dedicating your time and energy to raise vital funds. Whether by running, walking, cycling, fighting, cutting hair, or rallying others to give, you have carried this cause forward with love and purpose.

We want to recognise and thank every single one of you who has created and supported JustGiving campaigns since we began. Your efforts not only raise money but also raise awareness, leaving a legacy of strength and hope.

Just Giving Fundraising Campaigns and Challenges to date :

· Listen Up Manchester – Kate Rackham
· Kate Rackham Legacy Fund
· Archie Mayer – Charity Football Match
· Lynsey Evans – Marathon
· Lesley Theodorus & Amanda Unsworth / Trinity Logistics
· St Joseph's School – Staff Fundraiser
· Joe Nyland – Charity Fight
· Em & Lu – Half Marathon (for Kate)
· Michelle Gibb – Manchester Marathon (for Kate)
· Lauren Zawadzki – Manchester Half Marathon (for Kate)
· Shutt/Jones Family – Welly Walk
· Shelley Douglas & Caroline – Bike Ride
· Tom Waldron – Coast to Coast (for Kate)
· Woody Jones – Triathlon
· Kerri & Nat – Manchester 10k (for Kate)
· Emma Elmerhebi – Manchester Marathon (for Kate)
· Tom Redfern – Ultra MMA Derby
· Karen Eggleton
· Caroline & Jen – Manchester 10k
· Claire Starkey (for Kate)
· Joanne & Rob Harding – Great Manchester Run (for Kate)
· Leah Kirkham
· Nicola De Sousa – Cutting Hair
· Lorna Parkes
· Jodie Doyle
· Jennifer Delaney

- Stacey Smithies
- Emma Morley
- Max Randerson
- Lisa Molloy
- Daniel Heldreich
- Janet Williamson
- Emma Ballard-East
- Jodi Holland
- Jonathon McKeown
- Rebecca Rooney
- Charlotte Shutt, Woody Jones & Olivia Jones

THE 48 MILERS

A heartfelt thank you to Ann Bennet, Jean Todd, and Rosalie Galvin – lovingly known as The 48 Milers.

Your incredible dedication and endurance in taking on such a remarkable challenge is an inspiration to us all. The miles you walked were more than just steps on a journey – they were symbols of strength, solidarity, and the power of friendship. You have left a lasting mark on our community and on the legacy of this cause.

GoGreen
Office Solutions

FIGHTING

FIGHTING

We can't fight for our lives.
We are incurable.
We are fighting to be heard.
Fighting for a voice for the 61,000 patients living with secondary breast cancer in the UK.
Fighting to raise awareness and offering financial support and friendship for those living with incurable secondary breast cancer

BUZZCOCKS
FIGHTING

Liverpool FC

NRA

FIGHTING
TO BE
HEARD

FIGHTING

trinity
LOGISTICS LIMITED
Date: 31st MAY 2024
Fighting To Be Heard
£ 28783.24
Trinity Logistics Limited
FIGHTING TO BE HEARD
We can't fight for our lives. We are incurable. We are fighting to be heard.
Fighting for a voice for the 61,000 patients living with secondary breast cancer in the UK
Fighting to raise awareness and offering financial support and friendship for those living with incurable secondary breast cancer
MMA
ENTER THE CAGE AT AN INCREDIBLE EVENT
FREE TRAINING
RAISE FOR CHARITY
8 WEEKS
Making a difference
Crosby
Friendship
Financial support
Fighting to be Heard
THANK YOU FOR YOUR SUPPORT
Checkouts

Making a difference in Crosby
FIGHTING
Making a difference in Crosby
FIGHTING
FIGHTING
FIGHTING TO BE HEARD
Argos
BIG RED

659
FIGHTING TO BE HEARD
We can't fight for our lives.
We are incurable.
We are fighting to be heard.
Fighting for a voice for the 61,000
Fighting to raise awareness and offering financial support and friendship for those living with incurable secondary breast cancer.
Date 17.01.25
Pay Fighting to be Heard
Two thousand & ninety five pounds only
£ 2095.00

ACKNOWLEDGMENTS

The photoshoot, our charity, and the many events we have brought to life would not have been possible without the extraordinary talents, generosity, and belief of so many individuals and organisations.

Photographers

· Sane Seven – for capturing the powerful "Fighting to be Heard" image that has become an iconic symbol of our journey. Subsequent edited version. Gifting the copyright to Kate Orr.

· Jazmin Sinclair – for your beautiful photo shoot of the ladies in T-shirts, showcasing their strength and unity.

· Jonathan Oakes – for your inspiring International Women's Day shoot, celebrating the Power of Women through your lens.

· Ray Farley – for capturing the memorable images at the Power of Women event.

· Andrew AB – for your creative photography and support throughout this journey.

Creative Contributors

· Doll Beauty, Danielle Gregory, and Samantha Allen – for your generosity, artistry, creative input, and for gifting to support our mission.

· Lola's Lashes – for bringing the lashes that added beauty and confidence to our event.

· Nikki Craven – for your exceptional hair styling.

· Sophie Campbell – for your beautiful makeup artistry.

· Uptown Funk Makeovers – for your creativity and glamour.

· House of Vanity – for helping us prepare and present our women with confidence and pride.

· Zoe Ellen – for your makeup artistry.

· Holly Atherton – for your hair styling expertise.

· Ava May Tobin – MUA

· Roisin Pelan – Fightypants Creative – for designing our Fighting to be Heard logo, the Signs and Symptoms leaflet, and for the jackets that became a symbol of unity and strength.

· Rachel Faye – No Logo Designs - for your support with social content and your creativity has made a difference since you joined as a treasured volunteer.

26th September Photo Shoot Dream Team

· Charlie Foy, Sadie McKay & Ava may Tobin

· Influencer, model, supply liaison

· Planning

· Social / Design

Supporters & Champions

Seema Malhotra – for your unwavering support, from the very first day of the billboard campaign through to the International Women's Day Shoot and beyond. You have enabled us to launch on The Real Housewives of Cheshire, building awareness, sharing our mission, and collaborating with us every step of the way. By attending our events, opening doors, and bringing the press and celebrities with you, you have helped ensure our voices are heard far and wide. Most of all, thank you for being 100% behind us – always showing up, always championing the cause, and always standing alongside us with generosity and belief. Also, not to forget Jaya and Rae what a team.

Professional Support
· Colin Croft, Accountant – Matthews Sutton & Co Ltd – for your expertise and generosity in giving your time freely.
· Euan Fleming, Legal Formation Advisor – for your invaluable advice and commitment, offered freely to support our mission.
Clare Morgan – CEO of YKids for your generosity and guidance, thank you.
So many companies we owe so much - Vinci, Sesame Bankhall Group, Print Rooms, Clarity Creation, MGL World, Insurance With, Vinci and so many more.

Entertainment & Public Figures
· Leanne Campbell – for being with us from the very beginning of this journey and bringing your energy, heart and talent.
· Pauline Daniels – actress and comedian, for lending your talent and spirit.
· Danielle McDermott – PT and author, for your inspiration and encouragement.
· Natasha Hamilton – Atomic Kitten member, for sharing your voice and support.
· Rosalie Galvin – for being with us every step of the way, gifting your voice to each occasion. Your performances have transformed moments into memories, filling our events with magic, warmth, and emotion. The beauty and sincerity of your singing have lifted spirits, united people, and created unforgettable experiences. You have given not just your talent but your heart, and in doing so you have become a treasured part of our story.
· Charlotte Rose – the talented daughter of our trustee and founder, Nikki Williams. Charlotte has not only shared her voice and acting skills but also brought the pride of family into our journey.

Her artistry, passion, and dedication reflect the strength and inspiration of the women who stand behind this charity, making her contribution even more meaningful.

THIS IS ME EVENT SPONSORS

Our heartfelt thanks to the organisations who made the This Is Me event possible through their generous sponsorship. Your belief in our mission and your support allowed us to bring this vision to life.

Headline Sponsors
· MJ Quinn Limited
· FPC

Gold Sponsors
· Carpenters
· RopeWalks Hotel
· Minta Medical
· Brabners
· Blue Sky Foundation
· Applied Nutrition

Silver Sponsors
· Clarity Creation / MJL
· Standard Marketing Group
· My Planet Liverpool
· 7 Harrington Street Chambers
· Vibe HR
- Community Foundations for Lancashire and Merseyside
- Insurance With

ACKNOWLEDGEMENT TO MY DAUGHTER, AVA MAY TOBIN

To my incredible daughter, Ava May Tobin – a gifted marketing graduate who has not only designed the layout of this entire book but also poured her creativity into shaping our wider story. From creating social content to running the entire "This is Me" campaign for both our socials and the event, your dedication has been nothing short of extraordinary.

Thank you for your patience in managing this project around my time constraints and tiredness. You are brilliant. You have made your entire family so proud, and this book will always stand as the best business card you could ever hand out for your future.

I know how much all of these women mean to you, and I know how difficult it has been because you too have lost them after becoming so close. Yet, you have carried that weight with such courage, turning your grief into something that honours them beautifully.

Kate R, Gill, Kate E, and Sal would be so proud of you, just as everyone in this book is. And so am I. Thank you, Ava, for your love, your talent, and for making this possible.

Love You Mum x

"Our lives matter just as much as someone with a primary breast cancer diagnosis- yet people living with secondary breast cancer are treated like a footnote in the statistics. We are not a negative statistic. We are patients, parents, partners, friends, and workers whose lives deserve equal attention, equal research, equal access to trials and equal compassion."

Laura Shutt

WOMEN FEATURED IN ORIGINAL IMAGE

Sarah Larner
Kate Rackham
Emily Roberts
Jackie
Sally Nyland
Cathy Snape
Jeannie Ambrose
Gill Cory
Suzanne Williamson
Lisa Fleming
Lisa Jones
Laura Bailey
Lizzie England
Vicky Keating
Nikki Williams
Natalie Woodward
Kimberley Noble
Roisin Pelan
Fran Whitfield
Lesley Grainey